Turning Text into Gold

Taxonomies and Textual Analytics

Bill Inmon

Technics Publications

Published by:

2 Lindsley Road
Basking Ridge, NJ 07920 USA

https://www.TechnicsPub.com

Edited by Sadie Hoberman and Lauren McCafferty

First Printing 2017
Copyright © 2017 by Bill Inmon

ISBN, print ed.	9781634621663
ISBN, Kindle ed.	9781634621670
ISBN, ePub ed.	9781634621687
ISBN, Audio ed.	9781634621700

Library of Congress Control Number: 2016958935

This book is dedicated to my excellent friend – Georgia Burleson.
Georgia is what we should all aspire to.

Contents

Introduction

Multiple millennia ago, mankind set out to create wealth by turning everyday substances into gold. This was early alchemy, and ultimately it did not work. Despite the best minds and the best efforts, no one succeeded to transform other substances into gold because gold is an element. You can discover gold, you can dig for gold, and you can pan for gold, but you cannot create gold.

But the world has changed. Today we have a type of "modern alchemy" that *really* can create gold.

Text is the common fabric of society. Business is transacted in text, arguments are made in text, court cases are conducted in text, conversations between best friends transpire through text. In short, text is the medium of exchange between people living on earth.

Since the beginning of computing, text has defied the computer. Text is simply the original square peg in the round hole. Computer processes focus on structured transactions (not text).

For most of its early history, the computer was not much help in dealing with text. That was a shame, as some of the most important information was in the form of text.

But today, there exist advancements in technology that allow the computer to read, store and analyze text. And in doing so, a whole world of informed decision-making is possible. Unlike the alchemists of yore, if you know what you are doing, you really can turn text into gold.

As more and more applications were built, computer scientists realized that in order to manage those applications, an abstraction was needed. Enter the data model: an abstraction of computer applications. Furthermore, someone eventually observed that there was a lot of valuable data found in the text. In order to capture and use that text, the technology known as textual disambiguation was developed. Finally, at the intersection of data models and textual disambiguation, it dawned on computer scientists that an abstraction of text was needed.

Enter taxonomies.

Taxonomies have been around for a long time – long before the first computer was built or even conceived. But it is in the world of computation, where users must come to grips with text, that taxonomies have found a truly novel and important use.

Speech is complex. We are taught speech by our parents at a young age, and mimic it even before then. Adult brains process speech in a largely automated manner. But the automatic processing that occurs in our brain masks the complexity of speech.

Taxonomies (classifications) are critical to the processing of text. If we wish to get computers to process data like the brain does, then we need taxonomies. Sure, there is more to processing text than resolving text using taxonomies. But for most text, taxonomical resolution is the first step to making text useful.

This book will introduce you to the concept of taxonomies and how they are used to simplify and understand text.

This book is a practical book. Very little theory is discussed. Instead, the emphasis is on the practical aspects and usages of taxonomies, and the subsequent usage of taxonomies as a basis for textual analytics.

This book is for students of computer science, managers who have to deal with text, programmers who need to understand taxonomies, systems analysts who need to understand how to get business value out of a body of text, and especially those who are struggling to decode data lakes. Hopefully for those individuals (and many more), this book will serve as both an introduction to taxonomies and a guide to how taxonomies can be used to bring text into the realm of corporate decision-making.

WHI, Castle Rock, Co 1/1/2017

1: Brief History of Taxonomies

The earliest references to the study and creation of taxonomies (then called "classifications") come from the Greek philosophers. In particular, Aristotle was said to have used taxonomies to understand the world. Indeed the very origins of what we call science today hark back to Aristotle's practice of classifying objects.

It is said that Aristotle sorted animals into three basic classes: land animals, ocean animals, and air animals. Today we classify animals genetically, but does this mean that Aristotle got it wrong? Not at all. The classification used by Aristotle and the genetic classifications used today merely illustrate that there are different ways to classify things. Depending on the objective, there are many ways to create a classification, and each method is as correct as any other.

Aristotle's techniques of classification were carried on by scientists in later years. Darwin and Linnaeus used classification as a basic tool in their works in the field of biology. Linnaeus said that the first step in wisdom is to know the things themselves. In order to get this true familiarity with the objects in question, they must be distinguished from one another and given appropriate names and assigned to appropriate classifications.

Clearly, taxonomies are not new constructions, and their utility was understood by many important scholars throughout the ages. In the modern age, our increasing desire to understand text in the context of the computer has brought taxonomies renewed attention.

The first computers ran simple applications. Before long, the computer ran online transactions. Once the computer was used for online transactions, it was quickly weaved inexorably into the fabric of business. The day-to-day activities of many different institutions began to increasingly depend on the computer. Businesses hinged on online reservations, bank teller processing, manufacturing control systems, billing systems, and many more applications.

In a relatively short amount of time, the computer went from being a curiosity to an important component of everyday commerce. Throughout this revolution, one of the backbones of the computer was the DBMS (database management system). The DBMS required that data be organized into small, discrete, tightly defined elements called "records". Records were ideal for the storage of the information in transactions. The same type of transaction was repeated over and over and a record of each transaction was stored in the computer.

So monotonous were these transaction-based records that they began to be called "structured" data. The computer was capable of handling huge amounts of transaction records at a furious pace. Before long, managers were making important corporate decisions based on insights gleaned from this structured data.

INSUFFICIENCY OF STRUCTURED DATA

This decision-making based on structured data remained the status quo for some time, as it served businesses well. But eventually organizations found an anomaly. Business users soon found that there was a lot more data in their organizations than what they were using. In fact, organizations were only using a fraction of their data, as illustrated in this figure:

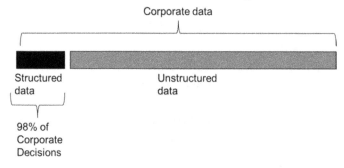

From any standpoint, this diagram simply does not make good business sense. While there is nothing wrong with structured data, there is clearly a lot more information that should be used to make decisions.

After this revelation, a few pioneers began to explore the possibilities of this vast tract of unstructured data.

They found that unstructured data could be classified into two types: textual and non-textual. The non-textual unstructured data came from a wide variety of sources: analog manufacturing data, meteorological data, measurement data, and more.

Along the way, analysts also discovered that there was a very high degree of business value to be found in textual data, compared to the low degree of business value of non-textual unstructured data. Typical examples of low value non-textual data are machine-generated analog data and even log tape data.

Because processing was concerned with unlocking business value, attention was turned to textual data. Indeed, in textual data was found such information as:

- Conversations with customers in call centers
- Corporate contracts
- Medical records
- Customer feedback for hotels and restaurants
- Safety logs
- Marketing feedback
- Emails

This division of unstructured data can be depicted graphically as follows:

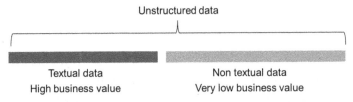

It was clear that textual data needed to be utilized, but there was a basic problem. Textual data simply did not fit into any form or pattern that was useful to the computer.

MANUAL PROCESSING

The first approach to address this dilemma was a manual one. Simply, a human being could read the text and turn it into a more structured form. The human being was flexible and did not require programming, and he or she could start immediately on reading and analyzing the text. But companies that tried this approach soon discovered that human beings:

- Had to be paid. They were expensive.

- Weren't reliable. Human being sometimes got sick, took holidays, and needed breaks.

- Made mistakes. After looking at text that was repetitious, the accuracy rate of the humans disintegrates.

- Lost efficiency. When they got tired, their work rate slowed down and their inaccuracies increased.

In short, humans were not the ideal tools to solve this problem. A manual approach proved impractical.

EVOLUTION OF TEXTUAL ANALYTIC TECHNOLOGY

Once the manual approach was abandoned, analysts tried to use technology to turn text into a form that could be analyzed by computers. There were a variety of methods explored:

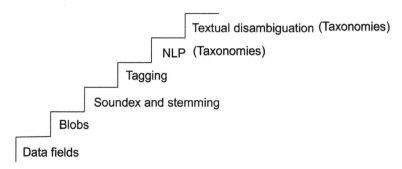

Although each of these efforts ultimately proved futile, it's worthwhile to understand the evolution that eventually led to the technology we use today.

The first attempt to get a handle on text was to create data fields in records that were reserved for text fields. These fields were often known as "comments" fields, where the user could insert any data they wished. The problem with comments was that the field length had to be large enough to accommodate the largest amount of text that someone would want to enter. The average comment length was never close to the maximum field length, so much storage space was wasted.

Database vendors recognized this mismatch between text length and field size, and responded with a structured type of data called a "blob". With a blob, the text could be any length; byte fit was no longer a problem because we no longer had to reserve the maximum field length. But blobs had their own problems. Once inside the blob, it was almost impossible to do anything with the text. There was no ability to search or index the text, or identify key values. Blobs ultimately solved one problem only to make obvious a more complex problem.

The practice of using "Soundex" and "stemming" was the first real attempt at pulling meaningful information out of text. Soundex involved placing an artificial value on words based on the sound of the word. For example, the name "William" might be encoded as "W445", where the first letter of the name is retained, vowels are dropped, and the letter "L" is replaced with a "4" and "M" with a "5". The goal of Soundex was to match words despite minor differences in spelling.

Similarly, stemming was the practice of reducing a word to its Greek or Latin stems. For example, the words "moved", "moving", "mover", and "move" can all be reduced to the common root stem of "mov". Stemming was done either algorithmically or by table lookup; either way, it had limited utility.

The next step in the quest to automatically analyze text was the practice of tagging. When a document was "tagged", the words were read and certain words were recognized and labelled.

Tagging was a big step in the right direction, but it wasn't quite enough. Tagging required a reader to know what they were looking for before they went to look for it. This need to presuppose the contents of text was a serious drawback. Furthermore, there were many forms of text that could not be caught by tagging. Tagging is good for identifying words, but not the context of words. Where context is an issue (which is almost everywhere), tagging is of limited value.

Natural language processing (or NLP) emerged as a solution to the problems of tagging. NLP made use of general purpose technologies such as taxonomies. This was really the first usage of taxonomies for the purpose of analyzing text. NLP was useful for such tasks as sentiment analysis. But as improved as NLP was, it still was limited in its usefulness.

Taxonomies were also used in the practice of textual disambiguation, the next step toward automatic text analysis. Textual disambiguation emphasized the importance of context, and employed a wide variety of techniques (other than taxonomical resolution) to reduce text to a state where it could be analyzed.

2: Simple Taxonomies

Again, a taxonomy is by simplest definition a classification. This doesn't mean, though, that taxonomies are always simple. They can have very complex characteristics. This chapter will introduce the basics of taxonomies, before we dive into their more complicated iterations. The first observation to be made about taxonomies is that there are many of them – almost an infinite number. There are taxonomies about science. About people. About animals. About ethics. About religion. Although "infinity" is never truly reachable, the number of taxonomies that could exist in the world comes close.

In order to begin the discussion on taxonomies, let's start with an example of a simple taxonomy (also known as a flat taxonomy):

Cars

      Ford

      Chevrolet

      Porsche

      Volkswagen

      Toyota

      Honda

      Kia

There is no such thing as a "right" or "wrong" taxonomy. There are taxonomies that are more appropriately applied to any given subject, sure, but they're not necessarily more correct than others. There are also taxonomies that are improperly structured, but that doesn't make them wrong.

TAXONOMY COMPONENTS

The subject of this taxonomy is *cars*. The types of cars are Ford, Chevrolet, Porsche, Volkswagen, Toyota, Honda, and Kia. The subject of the taxonomy is called the "generic text". The specific examples of text include Ford, Chevrolet, Porsche, Volkswagen, Toyota, Honda, and Kia.

The unnamed discriminator of this taxonomy is that all elements need to be a type of car. It would be inappropriate to put a Sherman tank, Boeing 747, Navajo blanket, bull elephant, or basking shark into this taxonomy because they are not types of cars. Only types of cars belong in this taxonomy. There are plenty of other car types that could have been placed into this taxonomy: Buick, DeSoto, Ferrari, or Dodge would have also fit. There could have been many reasons why a car brand was not placed in the taxonomy. The taxonomist could have only been concerned with fuel-efficient cars or car brands that were mentioned in a specific book. These reasons may be known only to the architect shaping the taxonomy. Note that the elements in this taxonomy could appear in other taxonomies. Specific elements are not exclusive to a given taxonomy.

There could exist the following taxonomy on Japanese products. The fact that Toyota and Honda appear in this taxonomy do not affect the validity of the first taxonomy. Toyota can be both a type of car and a Japanese product at the same time.

Japanese products
```
Toyota
Honda
sushi
Kikkoman sauce
motorcycle
kimono
Sapporo beer
```

Also note that a taxonomy can contain plurals. Usually a taxonomy references singular items, but on occasion it may be useful for plurals to be included:

Animals
```
cat
cats
dog
dogs
squirrel
squirrels
fish
deer
```

Another feature of a taxonomy is that when the taxonomy contains a verb, it may or may not contain derivatives of the base verb (such as present participles or past participles). This taxonomy does contain verb derivatives:

Action
```
move
moving
moved
run
runs
ran
running
```

When a taxonomy does not contain derivatives of a verb, the taxonomy usually makes use of stemming. Furthermore, a taxonomy may or may not contain negatives. This taxonomy contains negatives:

Tennis
```
        served
        not serve
        return
        not return
        faulted
        not fault
```

When a taxonomy does not contain negatives, another type of processing called "negative inference processing" can help. For example, take the sentence "I do not like ice cream and cake." The inference is that not only do I not like ice cream but I also don't like cake. The inference spans from the moment a sentiment is expressed to the designation of the end of sentence, which is usually a period.

Another feature of a taxonomy is that it can contain reference numbers. This taxonomy contains reference numbers:

Car
```
        Ford 5682
        Chevrolet 3652
        Porsche 9013
        Volkswagen 8729
        Toyota 8134
        Honda 2541
        Kia 8726
```

The reference numbers shown in this taxonomy can refer to many things, including industry reference numbers, internal reference numbers, or document numbers. In medicine, for instance, the numbers may refer to diagnostic codes.

Now that we've looked at several examples, we'll summarize the basic elements of any taxonomy:

- The taxonomy name, or the generic name
- The specific element name
- The discriminating criteria
- Reference numbers (optional)

The discriminating criteria can be identical in some taxonomies:

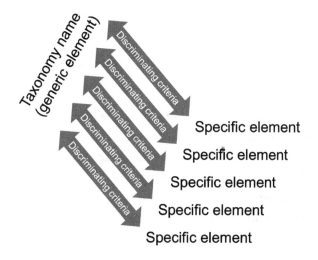

There can be many specific elements in a taxonomy, but each of those elements must satisfy the same discrimination criteria. Note that there must be at least one specific element in a taxonomy.

TAXONOMIES AND LANGUAGE

One of the interesting characteristics of a taxonomy is that the same taxonomy can exist in multiple languages. Here is the same taxonomy in multiple languages, in this case English and Spanish:

Plant	Planta
tree 20	árbol 20
flower 56	flor 56
bush 34	arbusto 34
grass 26	hierba 26
corn 31	maiz 31
nettle 18	ortiga 18

If the analyst wants to make a translation from one taxonomy to the other, they can use the reference number seen to the right of the specific element. On occasion, there are not precise translations of terms from one language to the next. In this case, the analyst uses the most logical translation that is available.

Another important note on language is that taxonomies can contain language that some may consider offensive. It is the job of the taxonomy to represent all language. Therefore it is inevitable that a properly-built taxonomy will contain language that is offensive in some circles. The architect creating the taxonomy would be remiss to not include all language, however coarse it might be.

More features sometimes seen in taxonomies are definitions and descriptions. In scientific journals, for instance, definitions and descriptions are often used, because most readers won't be familiar with the specialized language. In business, though, terms and words are usually less esoteric. Taxonomies in the realm of business, therefore, usually don't include definitions.

3: Complex Taxonomies

Simple taxonomies are useful and quite common, but as was mentioned earlier, they're only the tip of the taxonomy iceberg.

Generally speaking, there are three types of taxonomies: flat (or simple) taxonomies, hierarchical taxonomies, and networked taxonomies.

To review, here is a flat or simple taxonomy:

Car
```
        Ford
        Honda
        Buick
        Toyota
        Volkswagen
```

A flat taxonomy has only one level of dependencies. In a flat taxonomy there are generic classes of data, each one having one level of specific occurrences.

Here is a graphic depiction of the flat taxonomy:

HIERARCHICAL TAXONOMIES

The second type of taxonomy is a hierarchical taxonomy. A hierarchical taxonomy has multiple levels of dependencies.

Here is an example of a hierarchical taxonomy:

```
Car
        Ford
                Mustang
        Buick
                LeSabre
        Toyota
                Prius
        Volkswagen
                Beetle
                Bus
```

Note that in a hierarchical taxonomy, there can be any number of levels of dependency.

Here is a graphic depiction of a hierarchical taxonomy:

You may have noticed that two or more simple taxonomies can be combined to form a hierarchical relationship between taxonomies. A hierarchical relationship is natural for many forms of data.

For example, there is a relationship between the taxonomy for country and state, and another relationship between state and city. Indeed there are many, many examples of hierarchical relationships between data that are represented by taxonomies.

A lengthy set of relationships can be constructed between different taxonomies:

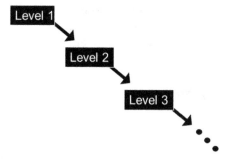

The following figure shows the simple relationship between the different taxonomies. The specific element of USA in the country taxonomy relates to the specific element of Texas found in the state taxonomy. The city of Dallas in the city taxonomy relates to the state of Texas in the example. In such a fashion a hierarchical relationship between taxonomies is formed:

```
Country
        Canada          State
        Mexico          Louisiana       City
        USA    ───────> Texas ──┐       El Paso
        Chile           New Mexico └──>  Dallas
        Argentina       Colorado        Sante Fe
        Peru            California      Sacramento
        Brazil          Oregon          Portland
                                        Tacoma
                                        Boise
```

Here is a graphical depiction of the hierarchical relationship between country and state and city:

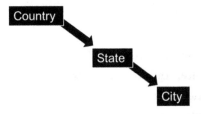

How does the analyst make the connections between country and state, and between state and city, using the data found in the previous example? There is no data within the taxonomies that makes obvious these connections.

The implication is that an independent lookup must be done to make the connection when the data is arranged as shown.

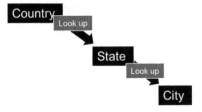

One of the really nice aspects of the data found in this hierarchical relationship is that it is simple and clean. There are plenty of other examples that are not simple and clean. Take for example a man's name: Dean. Dean can be a first name, a last name, or even a title. Or consider the relationship between piston and motor. Piston relates to motor, but only indirectly. The drawback here is the complexity of the lookup processing that is required.

EMBEDDED RELATIONSHIPS

We can also have a taxonomy where the data necessary to identify the relationship is included (or embedded) in the taxonomy itself:

```
Country
    Canada       State
    Mexico       Louisiana (USA)      City
    USA          Texas (USA)          El Paso (Texas)
    Chile        New Mexico (USA)     Dallas (Texas)
    Argentina    Colorado (USA)       Sante Fe (New Mexico)
    Peru         California (USA)     Sacramento (California)
    Brazil       Oregon (USA)         Portland (Oregon)
                                      Tacoma (Washington)
                                      Boise (Idaho)
```

As you can see, each specific element is followed by additional data that indicates its relationship to other taxonomies.

Because the relationships are made obvious, this taxonomy is relatively simple and streamlined to process. But the taxonomy requires considerably more data management. The relationships have to be correct. In addition, if there is any chance that the relationships will change, then maintenance to the taxonomies is needed.

In the case shown, states do not typically change countries and cities do not change states, so there is little or no maintenance required. But if there were changes in the basic relationship itself, the taxonomies reflecting the relationships would have to change.

There is a tradeoff, then, between the simplicity of the structure and the background processing required to use the data. This tradeoff is a classic one that is found many places in information processing.

Instead of doing a lookup to identify relationships, we can use an embedded key:

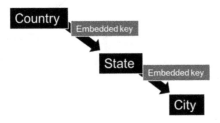

For example, in the taxonomy for state, the country key could be embedded. The result would look like:

```
Texas (USA)
New Mexico (USA)
Colorado (USA)
Utah (USA)
```

As a rule, an embedded key is much easier to access than an independent look up, assuming the embedded key has been created properly.

RECURSIVE TAXONOMIES

There is yet another alternative to using taxonomies to implement a hierarchical relationship. That alternative can be called the "recursive option".

In the recursive option there is only one taxonomy. In this example the taxonomy could be named "geographic region". There are different types of geographic regions represented within the taxonomy. One type of geographic region is country. Another is state. Another is city. Here is an example of the recursive option for the creation of a taxonomy:

```
Geographic region
        country – USA
        state – Texas (USA)
        city – Dallas (Texas)
        state – New Mexico (USA)
```

```
city - Santa Fe (New Mexico)
city - Albuquerque (New Mexico)
state - Nevada (USA)
city - Reno (Nevada)
```

Different types of geographic regions are contained in the taxonomy, and there exist relationships among the different elements. Each state points to a country, and each city points to a state.

Choosing the recursive depiction of taxonomies has benefits and drawbacks. From a system standpoint, a benefit is that only one taxonomy is needed; other representations require multiple taxonomies. If you don't use a recursive structure, you need a different taxonomy for each level of the hierarchy. Dealing with one data definition is always easier than juggling multiple definitions. The primary drawback of recursive representations is the fact that processing can become complex. For example, suppose you have a recursive taxonomy and all you want to look for are states. One way or the other, you need the ability to skip over and not process cities and countries.

Here is a taxonomy that has elements that point back into each other:

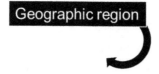

NETWORKED TAXONOMIES

The third type of taxonomy is the networked taxonomy. In a networked taxonomy, the same specific term can be classified multiple ways. Here is an example of a networked taxonomy:

Car	German products	Japanese products
Ford	sausage	sushi
Honda	clocks	soy sauce
Buick	Volkswagen	Samurai swords
Toyota	Porsche	Toyota
Volkswagen	schnitzel	Honda

Here is a graphical depiction of a networked taxonomy:

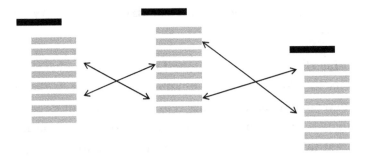

Each of the three types of taxonomies has its own place in textual analytic processing. Flat taxonomies are used for simple textual analytic processing, such as in call center analysis. Hierarchical taxonomies are used for the processing of more complex documents, such as contracts or books. Networked taxonomies are used where there are multiple ways of viewing the same textual data.

MORE APPLICATIONS OF TAXONOMIES

One of the features of taxonomies is that in almost every case, multiple taxonomies can be used to process a body of text. For example, suppose the subject of the text were automobile manufacturing. The taxonomies that typically would be chosen might include automotive bill of material processing, manufacturing materials, car distribution, and retail pricing for automobiles. Multiple taxonomies are chosen to process automotive text:

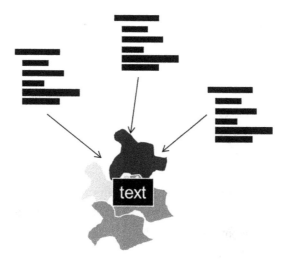

There is no theoretical limit as to how many taxonomies can be chosen for processing a body of text. However, there is one criterion that must be met by all taxonomies utilized: there must be a business relationship between the body of text and the taxonomy.

For example, suppose that the body of text were about automotive manufacturing. It would be very unusual to find taxonomies on religion, home schooling, Thanksgiving recipes, or submarine warfare used against the automotive text.

Suppose there were three taxonomies that were being used to process a body of text. It is possible to arrange the taxonomies so that one of them is a "preferred" taxonomy. When it is time to process a block of text, the preferred taxonomy is processed first. If the term being sought is found in the preferred taxonomy, no other processing is done. But if no hits are made on the preferred taxonomy, then the remaining taxonomies are searched.

It is normal for the name of the taxonomy to be included as a specific element, as in this example:

Airplane
```
airplane
propeller
wing
tail
rudder
flaps
cabin
```

In this case the name of the taxonomy is airplane. But in the specific elements for airplane, the word "airplane" appears again. Such a practice in the building of a taxonomy is absolutely normal and appropriate. From a mathematical standpoint, any element is always properly contained in its own superset.

We've already probed simple and complex taxonomies. But regardless of their construction or complexity, taxonomies can be described in other terms: as "generic" or "custom" taxonomies. A generic taxonomy is one where the elements of the taxonomy will be the same for every organization. A typical generic taxonomy could be the expression of taste. The generic expressions "I like", "I love", or "I admire" do not change from one company to the next. The customers of one company will use the same expressions as the customers of another company. Therefore the expression of sentiment is generic.

Custom taxonomies, on the other hand, are those taxonomies that are specific to a company. A restaurant may have a desserts taxonomy while a construction company may have a lumber taxonomy; it would be surprising to find either taxonomy in the other's business plans.

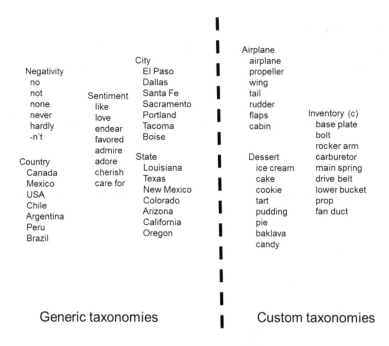

Negativity		City	Airplane	
no		El Paso	airplane	
not	Sentiment	Dallas	propeller	
none	like	Santa Fe	wing	
never	love	Sacramento	tail	
hardly	endear	Portland	rudder	
-n't	favored	Tacoma	flaps	Inventory (c)
	admire	Boise	cabin	base plate
	adore			bolt
Country	cherish	State		rocker arm
Canada	care for	Louisiana	Dessert	carburetor
Mexico		Texas	ice cream	main spring
USA		New Mexico	cake	drive belt
Chile		Colorado	cookie	lower bucket
Argentina		Arizona	tart	prop
Peru		California	pudding	fan duct
Brazil		Oregon	pie	
			baklava	
			candy	

Generic taxonomies   Custom taxonomies

When processing multiple taxonomies, it's possible to slip into a pattern called the "deadly embrace". This pattern is an infinite loop; only killing the program in execution can end it.

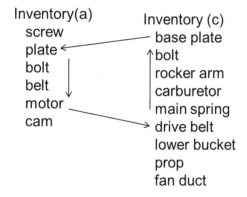

As an example of a deadly embrace, suppose that in the taxonomy for inventory(a) a plate is accessed. The processing of plate leads to the processing of motor in the same taxonomy. Next the drive belt in the taxonomy for inventory(c) is accessed. This processing leads to the processing of a base plate in inventory(c). Processing then continues to plate in inventory(a). In such a manner, the system is stuck.

When the programmer is developing the logic that will used to examine the elements found in a taxonomy, the programmer needs to guard against the execution of elements in the taxonomy that will lead to a deadly embrace.

A final specialized taxonomy is the negation taxonomy, as seen in this example for the English language:

```
Negation
      no
      not
      none
      never
      hardly
      neither
```

The negation taxonomy is used when negative inference processing is required. If a term's negative version is included alongside it within a taxonomy, then an additional negation taxonomy is not needed. If this is the case, though, it is necessary to include *all* negation terms that are possible. For this reason, the usage of a negative taxonomy is preferred in most circumstances.

4: Ontologies

Ontologies are not new; they've been around for as long as there has been philosophy. One of the earliest and most famous examples of ontology is Rene Descartes' declaration "cogito ergo sum," or "I think therefore I am". These "philosophical ontologies" are founded in existentialism and hotly debated by philosophers; in that context, they have rather esoteric meanings.

The ontology in the context of textual analytics, though, has a different and very precise definition. An ontology is a logical relationship of elements participating in a taxonomy. These incarnations of ontologies are only distantly related to the ontologies that are found in philosophy.

So what purpose does an ontology serve? In fact, the ontology has many uses. Perhaps the most important purpose of the ontology is to serve as a lens into the business of the organization.

In order to solve any business-related problems, analysts must understand the business and activities of the business environment. The ontology serves to give management, technicians, users, and anyone else a glimpse into the business environment. As such, the ontology becomes a bridge between the world of technology and the world of business and commerce. In a way, the ontology becomes the larger context for understanding the language of a particular business or commerce.

From a more technical perspective, the ontology serves the purpose of providing a framework for conducting textual analysis during the development and analysis process.

The analyst needs a framework for ensuring the accuracy and quality of the taxonomies. The ontology is precisely the framework that is needed. With the ontology it is easy to:

- Verify completeness of the taxonomies

- Verify consistency and alignment of the taxonomies

- Verify the business relevance of the taxonomies

In the world of textual analytics and taxonomies, there are two types of ontologies: an internal ontology and an external ontology.

An internal taxonomy is called "internal" because it can be created independently of any body of text. An external ontology is called "external" because it must have an external body of text to which the taxonomies are applied. An internal ontology must meet all of the following requirements:

- Consists of either two or more simple taxonomies, or a single recursive taxonomy.

- Contains one or more relationships among specific elements.

- Has a business relationship to the body of text.

Here is an example of an internal ontology:

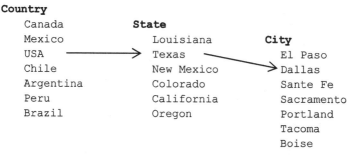

```
Country
    Canada          State
    Mexico              Louisiana       City
    USA     ──────────→ Texas               El Paso
    Chile               New Mexico    ─────→ Dallas
    Argentina           Colorado            Sante Fe
    Peru                California          Sacramento
    Brazil              Oregon              Portland
                                            Tacoma
                                            Boise
```

There are multiple taxonomies in this example: one for country, one for state, and one for city. There is a relationship of specific data elements to other specific data elements. And each of the taxonomies can be classified as a geographic boundary.

The data in this example satisfies the requirements for being an internal ontology. If an ontology is not internal, it must be external. An external ontology must meet all of the following requirements:

- Consists of either two or more simple taxonomies, or a single recursive taxonomy.

- Contains one or more relationships among specific data elements.

- Has a business relationship to the body of text.

In other words, an external taxonomy is an internal taxonomy that has been applied to text, and where inference processing is utilized.

Here is an example of an external ontology:

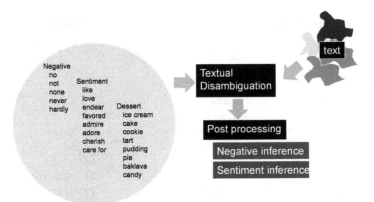

This example includes multiple simple taxonomies: negative, sentiment, and dessert. There are one or more relationships between the specific data elements. There is a clear business relationship between the taxonomies and the body of text; in this case, people have commented on their feelings about a dessert, probably in a restaurant. There is processing of the text. And there is inference processing that occurs against the results of the text that has been processed.

Therefore, this data meets the requirements to be considered an external taxonomy.

5: Obtaining Taxonomies

Taxonomies are essential parts of our language. Strictly speaking, taxonomies come from language itself. But where do we find the taxonomies that we need for successful textual analytics?

There are two basic sources of taxonomies that are useful for textual analytics:

- Prefabricated, curated taxonomies prepared by a taxonomy vendor

- Handmade, manually-prepared taxonomies

CURATED TAXONOMIES

There is a very strong case to be made for prefabricated, curated taxonomies. The basis for prefabricated, curated taxonomies stems from the fact that, for the most part, the taxonomies for one organization are going to be very, very similar to the taxonomies for another company in the same line of business.

Because of the similarity of taxonomies among similar companies, it makes sense that any industry-specific taxonomy be created once, and then distributed to the different companies that need it. This figure shows the building, curation, and distribution of taxonomies by a vendor of taxonomies:

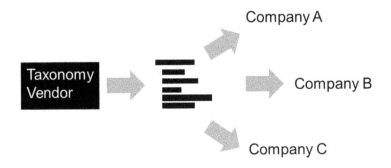

There are many reasons why the vendor distribution model makes sense. The first (and most important) reason is that it is wasteful for an organization to spend time and resources on something that has already been done. There is such an extreme case of similarity between the taxonomies of companies in the same line of business that it doesn't make sense for a company to "reinvent the wheel".

Additionally, there are special skills required in order to build a taxonomy. Most companies do not have a resident taxonomist as a standard employee.

Another reason why utilizing a taxonomy vendor is a good idea is that it puts the organization that purchases the taxonomy into the position of being an editor. Humans are much better at editing than writing. When a human sees what somebody else has done, the human is quick to make suggestions and improvements. Making suggestions is much easier and much more natural for most people than creating a document in the first place.

For these and more reasons, when a taxonomy is needed, it makes sense for most companies to simply acquire it from a taxonomy vendor. The taxonomies built by the vendor are sometimes called "prefabricated" or "curated" taxonomies.

Once the organization has acquired the curated taxonomy, a certain amount of customization is usually required.

As a rule, less than 5% of the terms and relationships found in the curated taxonomy should need to be customized. If more than 5% adjustment is needed, then the wrong curated taxonomy has been chosen.

It is normally the task of the analyst to choose exactly which taxonomies from the vendor are most appropriate. It is typical for the vendor to have far many more taxonomies than any one organization could use.

For example, suppose the body of text is about the Army. The taxonomies that are likely to be chosen include basic training, military organization, command and controls, and weaponry. It is unlikely that taxonomies that relate to surgery, or airplane operations, or football tactics would be chosen, even though the taxonomy vendor may have all of those taxonomies and more available.

BUILDING YOUR OWN TAXONOMY

In nearly every circumstance, it makes the most sense to utilize a vendor of taxonomies. However, sometimes you'll find yourself needing to create your own taxonomy.

The simplest way to build your own taxonomy is to start with a small subset of the body of text that you want to analyze. The general procedure is to work with a small amount of text, then go back and select another small amount of text, adding on to the results that have already been produced. In other words, an iterative approach is needed to attack the body of text that needs to be analyzed.

Here is a small amount of text that was chosen from airline complaints that are publicly available on the internet:

> I was denied a refund for baggage check charge of $25. I charged a companion ticket on my United Mileage Plus Explorer credit card for which I pay $95 a year. One of the benefits of having the card is to check your and your companion's bag free of charge. I submitted my refund request through United's online 'baggage refund' site. I was credited the $25 for the outbound trip, however, they denied the inbound charge.

The first step in analyzing the text is to identify primary words that have business significance. A primary word is a noun, and only the nouns that have business significance are chosen.

In this example, business-relevant nouns include:

> I was denied a refund for baggage check charge of $25. I charged a companion ticket on my United Mileage Plus Explorer credit card for which I pay $95 a year. One of the benefits of having the card is to check your and your companion's bag free of charge. I submitted my refund request through United's online 'baggage refund' site. I was credited the $25 for the outbound trip, however, they denied the inbound charge.

Business-relevant nouns:
```
Refund
charge
ticket
credit card
benefits
bag
site
trip
```

QUALIFYING THE NOUNS

The next step is to go back to the text and find what qualifiers exist that modify the business-relevant nouns. This usually amounts to identifying adjectives for the nouns:

I was denied a refund for baggage check charge of $25. I charged a companion ticket on my United Mileage Plus Explorer credit card for which I pay $95 a year. One of the benefits of having the card is to check your and your companion's bag free of charge. I submitted my refund request through United's online 'baggage refund' site. I was credited the $25 for the outbound trip, however, they denied the inbound charge.

Once this step is done, the qualifiers are added to the list of business-relevant nouns, attached to the nouns they modify:

Refund	**Credit card**	**Site**
	United MP Explorer	baggage refund
Charge		
baggage check	**Benefits**	
inbound		
	Bag	
	companion	

The process is repeated over and over with different occurrences of text. The iterative nature of creating the taxonomies from raw text is shown here:

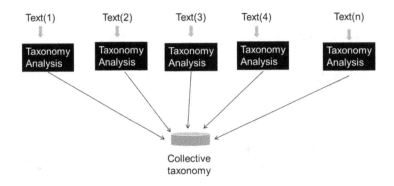

The process of collecting and assimilating words into the taxonomy is continued until we start to see a large degree of repetition (approximately 70% or more). When the new text you are processing starts to contain business relevant terms that already appear in the taxonomies, then you know you are finished.

Of course, there will always be some words that still need to be captured in the taxonomy. But doing the job with 90% accuracy usually is good enough, at least to get started down the path of textual analytics.

6: Changing Taxonomies

Consider the word "blog". If you would have said the word "blog" to anyone in the 1990's, nobody would have known what you were talking about. Today, though, the word "blog" is understood by many people.

The word "blog" is merely one example of the fact the language is constantly changing. These changes may occur slowly, but language nevertheless is dynamic. New words are added and older words fall into disuse so effortlessly and so gradually that we are hardly aware of the change.

Taxonomies are reflections of the language of the world; it is natural that as the world changes, taxonomies also change.

US States (1787)	US States (1788)
Delaware	Delaware
Pennsylvania	Pennsylvania
New Jersey	New Jersey
	Georgia
	Connecticut
	Massachusetts
	Maryland

Because of the constant changes in words and terminology, it is necessary to periodically update the taxonomies that are used in textual analytics. Taxonomies can be updated manually or taxonomies can be kept up to date by the taxonomy vendor.

As with the initial acquisition of the taxonomy, there are good reasons for allowing the taxonomy vendor to update the taxonomies. The main reason is that the taxonomy vendor is equipped to make the changes. If an organization attempts to manually maintain their own taxonomies, the organization must have a professional taxonomist on staff.

There is an issue that arises with the changing of taxonomies over time. Suppose an organization has a taxonomy, and on one given day, it processes text using that taxonomy. Now suppose that on the following day, the taxonomy has changed.

The organization now has a dilemma. It has text that has been processed under the original taxonomy, and text that needs to be processed the next day, using a slightly different taxonomy. What does the organization do about the text that has already been processed? There are two potential solutions.

One solution is to simply process the data on Day 2 using the new taxonomy, and leave the data from Day 1 as it was. Although there will exist two different versions of the output data, there are some benefits of this approach:

- No rerunning is required

- This solution is simplest

- There may be business reasons to not want to rerun the data

The second solution entails processing the Day 2 data using the new and updated Day 2 taxonomy, and also reprocessing the text from the previous day using the Day 2 taxonomy. Although potentially massive amounts of resources are required to reprocess the data, there are some benefits of this approach:

- The results are consistent with the latest taxonomy

- There may be business reasons to rerun all the data

Ultimately, the best solution depends on business circumstances. Each option comes with tradeoffs which must be weighed against the situation at hand and the business' needs.

7: Taxonomies as Databases

Taxonomies are used to organize text in order to create a database. But taxonomies are also themselves databases. The steps to bringing a vendor's taxonomy into the organization are:

Taxonomy
Vendor

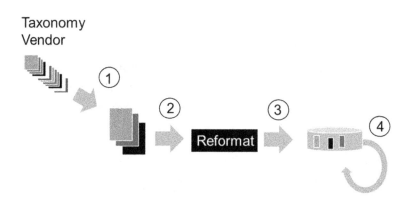

1. As previously discussed, the first step the organization takes is to select which taxonomies will be needed. The taxonomy vendor will have many more taxonomies than will be needed (or even be useful) to the

organization. If a taxonomy has business relevance then it is selected.

2. After the relevant taxonomies are selected from a vendor, they must be transformed into a format that is useful for textual disambiguation processing. If the organization is using a standard textual disambiguation package, the format is tailored to suit the needs of the package. If textual disambiguation is on a customized basis, the format of the taxonomies is shaped to fit the needs of the custom disambiguation system.

3. After reformatting, the taxonomies are gathered into the corporate taxonomy library. This is the database for taxonomies, similar to a data dictionary for definitions. Frequently, the corporate taxonomies are collected and managed by vendor-supplied software. However, it is not mandatory that such software be used. It is entirely possible to build a database manually.

4. The fourth step is to customize the taxonomies to suit the needs of the organization. For example, a car manufacturer may want to insert the actual brand names of their cars into their own taxonomy.

Once the taxonomies are prepared for use, they can be used for textual disambiguation. This graphic describes the architecture for processing taxonomies by textual disambiguation:

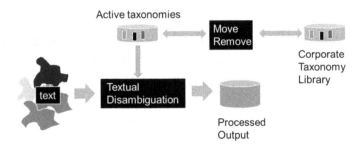

This figure shows that raw text goes through the process of textual disambiguation, along with taxonomies. The taxonomies that are used in processing are called the "active taxonomies". Typically an organization will have many more taxonomies than those that will be used in an active disambiguation of text. Textual disambiguation operates on only one type of text at a time; the taxonomies that are used actively are those that are relevant to the text being processed.

For example, suppose the raw text being processed is a selection of resumes from human resources. Only the taxonomies that directly relate to resumes will be actively used. The taxonomies for contracts, safety systems, or sentiment would not be used for processing resumes.

Because organizations will have many more taxonomies than are actively being used at one time, there is a need to separate the active taxonomies from the inactive taxonomies. As such, taxonomies reside in two different places. All taxonomies "live" in the corporate taxonomy library. When taxonomies are needed for active use in textual disambiguation, they move to the active taxonomy queue.

When textual disambiguation is complete, the analyst is left with processed output. The processed output is the text that has been rearranged into the form of a standard database management system. This output can be utilized by an analytical processer such as Tableau, Qlik, Excel, or SAS.

MoveRemove Processing

Taxonomies are moved to and from the active textual disambiguation process by means of a taxonomy management program called "MoveRemove". When a taxonomy is ready to be used by textual disambiguation, the MoveRemove program retrieves it from the corporate library and places it in the active queue.

Another important function of the MoveRemove program is to clean out the active taxonomy queue. Suppose you are working on a contracts project and, as such, your active taxonomy queue is full of taxonomies related to contracts. When you switch to working on a safety project, you no longer need these contract-related taxonomies. Before switching projects, you can use the MoveRemove program to remove the contract taxonomies from the active taxonomy queue, and move the safety-related taxonomies into the queue.

That's not all that the MoveRemove program can do. On occasion it is necessary to combine two or more taxonomies into a single taxonomy when moving taxonomies to the active queue. As an example of combining two taxonomies, suppose a corporation has a taxonomy for blue collar workers and another taxonomy for white collar workers. It may be entirely plausible to combine the taxonomies to create a general taxonomy for all workers.

The MoveRemove program can be used to load more than one taxonomy into the active queue creating a single taxonomy, as follows:

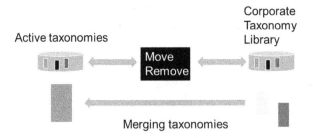

Taxonomy Customization

As mentioned earlier, once taxonomies have been added into the corporate taxonomy library, they must often be customized.

When the taxonomy vendor creates a taxonomy, it must be fairly generic. The taxonomy must be useable by many organizations, and so it must contain nonspecific terms, rather than specific product or brand names. Once acquired, though, the company usually wants the taxonomy to be more specific to its products and brands. Thus, it is normal for some customization to be needed.

There are many ways the taxonomy can be customized. One way is in terms of idioms. An example of an idiom is a taxonomy vendor calling some piece of building equipment a "re-bar" whereas the local terminology is a "re-rod".

Similarly, you may need to customize certain unique expressions. Your customers may use the expression "red hot" to mean that something is especially good, but perhaps the vendor had never heard that term. You can add "red hot" to your taxonomy of expressions of satisfaction.

Another customization function is that of changing spelling. Suppose the audience you are processing text for is a British audience. You could change the spelling of "color" to "colour". In such a fashion you could analyze the comments left using British dialect.

Yet another use of customization is to make the terminology fit your particular organization. Suppose your organization has a term "partno" which is taken to mean "part number". You could add "partno" to the taxonomy.

Another customization is plurality. Suppose the taxonomy vendor gives you a taxonomy with only singular references, like "bird", "car", and "steak". If there was a need to do so you could add "birds", "cars", and "steaks".

There are many more ways that a taxonomy can be customized as it is laced into the corporate taxonomy library, but these are some of the most common examples.

WORD PAIRS

When stored in a database, a taxonomy can always be broken into a set of "word pairs". Regardless of how complex a taxonomy may be, from the standpoint of computer storage, the taxonomy can always be expressed as a collection of pairs of items – one generic and one specific.

Here we see a hierarchical taxonomy that has been broken down into an ordered set of word pairs:

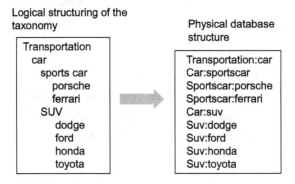

In this figure we can see both the taxonomy's hierarchical structure as well as its representation as an ordered set of word pairs.

In the list of ordered word pairs, a specific word becomes a generic word in the subsequent word pair, where it is paired with an even more specific word pair. For example, one word pair shows that a car can be a sports car. Then the next word pair shows that a sports car can be a Porsche.

In such a fashion the hierarchical nature of the taxonomy is preserved even when stored as an ordered set of word pairs.

Of course, when the ordered set of word pairs is read, the program must use logic to reconstruct the hierarchical nature of the taxonomy:

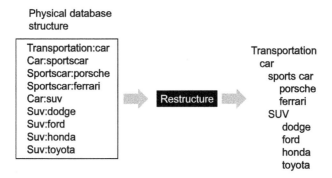

TRANSPORTING THE TAXONOMY

Sometimes it is necessary to send a taxonomy from one person to the next, or from one location to another. This transportation is easily accomplished as seen here:

Transferring a taxonomy from one user to the next

Here a taxonomy is removed from one corporate taxonomy library for User A. From there, the taxonomy is placed into a standard database, such as Excel, and is transported electronically to wherever it needs to go. Upon arrival it is taken from Excel and placed into the corporate taxonomy library of User B.

8: Taxonomies and Data Models

There are two very different paths of processing which, at first glance, do not intersect. These are known as the text-based path and the transaction-based path.

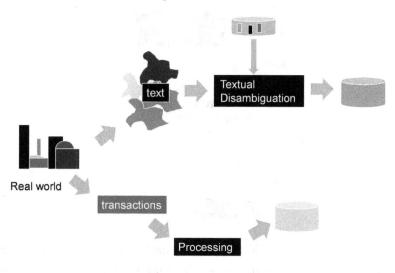

Both paths have the same starting point: activity in the real world. From there, in the text-based path, words (articles, contracts, emails, etc.) are written, and then processed into a text-based database.

We briefly discussed a transaction-based path earlier, in Chapter 1. This path is initiated when some online activity occurs. A check is cashed, a purchase is made, or a reservation is taken. Once the activity is completed, a record of the activity is created in the transaction-based database.

Despite the common origin, these two paths are very disparate.

An interesting question arises: can the data from the two paths be compared and contrasted?

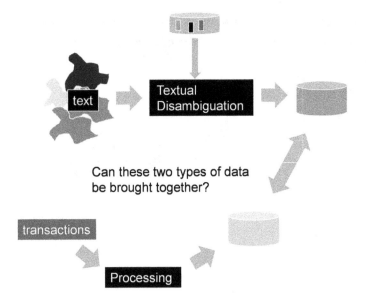

The key to being able to compare and contrast data from the different paths lies in the intellectual foundation of the two environments. The intellectual foundation of the text-based environment is the taxonomy. The intellectual foundation of the transaction based environment is the data model.

Note that the classical data model has been thoroughly discussed and documented in the industry. The brief description here is designed to merely acquaint the reader with some basic concepts. If there is a desire for further reading, there are many sources that are available.

The data model is an abstraction of the data found in the transaction database. The heart of the data model is the entity relationship diagram (ERD). The ERD identifies the major subject areas of the organization. Typical major subject areas include part, supplier, shipment, order, and the like. The major subject areas are represented by oval shapes in the ERD. If there is a direct relationship between the different entities, a line is drawn between the two entities participating in the relationship.

As a rule, the ERD is devoid of other details. The purpose of the ERD is simply to provide a high-level perspective of the data found in the database.

The next level of the data model is the data item set (DIS) level:

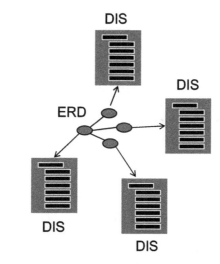

We see that each of the entities identified in the ERD has a corresponding DIS. The DIS contains a much more detailed description of the data found in the data model.

The DIS contains such important information as:

- Name of the table that will be created from the DIS

- Attribute name, such as name, address, sex, date of birth, telephone number, etc.

- Physical definition of the attribute, such as char(25), varchar(250), decimal(15,2), etc.

- Keys, such as part number, social security number, etc.

- Indexes, such as last name, car model type, age, place of birth, etc.

- Definitions

- Key/foreign key relationships

- Other relationships

The DIS determines the "layout" of the data found in the database. The ERD and all of the associated DIS constitute the data model. The database design is made from the data model.

There is a close resemblance between the data model and the taxonomy. The similarities are most obvious at the DIS to taxonomy level:

Clearly, the taxonomy name corresponds to the DIS table name. In addition, there is an approximate correspondence between the specific element found in the taxonomy and the attribute name found in the DIS.

Despite these similarities, there are some very fundamental differences between the two abstractions. For example, in the taxonomy there is no physical description of the data, nor are there any key/foreign key relationships.

The major discrepancy, though, lies in how the data gets from the real word to the output database. In the text-based model, data flows as follows:

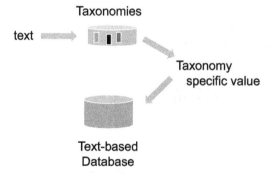

Text enters the system and is then passed against the contents of the taxonomy. The search looks for specific elements in the taxonomy. If there is a match with a specific element, the generic term is assigned to the word and a record is written to the text database.

As an example, consider a taxonomy for cars. In the raw text there is mention of the word "Porsche". The taxonomy recognizes Porsche as a car. In the text-based database, "car" is associated with the word "Porsche".

Data enters the transaction-based database in a very different manner. The first step to getting data into the transaction-based database is to design the structure of the database. The data model is used to shape the structure:

Data model

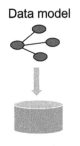

Transaction-based
Database

Once the database has been designed, applications can now execute against the database. It is during the execution of transactions that data finds its way into the database:

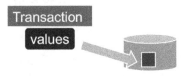

Transaction-based
Database

In order to better understand the interactions of taxonomies, data models and their respective databases, a more detailed example is required.

Suppose a reservation for an airplane flight is made in London, England. That reservation is made by transacting the appropriate data against the database:

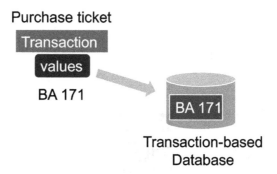

The purchase of a ticket is made. As a result of the purchase, a reservation is made on British Airways flight 171. The values reflecting the purchase of the ticket are entered into the database.

Now suppose the passenger takes the flight and has a complaint. The passenger writes the complaint to one of the online databases that are publicly available on the internet:

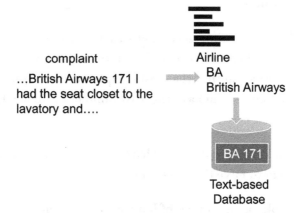

The text from the complaint is entered into the textual disambiguation program. The taxonomy used for airline complaints recognizes the text "British Airways". Textual extract, transform, and load (ETL) then writes out a record to the text-based database. Now that data has been placed into the two databases, it is possible to analytically process data from both the databases:

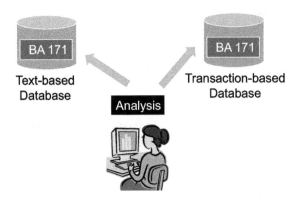

Once the analyst is able to use data from both databases simultaneously, a whole new world of analytics opens up. For instance, the analyst can start to:

- Look for patterns of behavior, such as passengers of British Airways always seeming to wait too long before boarding.

- Look at the intersection of structured and unstructured data using standard analytical tools, such as the observation that the most complaints come from customers who have the least number of frequent flyer miles.

- Look for exceptions, such as that flights to Singapore seem to have the most problems.

- Look for summaries of both structured and unstructured data, such as noting that the largest number of complaints come from passengers who traveled in January.

9: Types of Textual Data

There are two categories of textual data: structured and unstructured. Textual unstructured data bears no resemblance from one record or document of data to the next. A good example of textual unstructured data is email. When a person writes an email, the chances are very good that the email is unique. If an email turns out to be similar to another email, it is purely by happenstance.

The counterpart is textual structured data. Textual structured data is more predictable. In textual structured data, there is a strong resemblance from one document to the next.

An example of textual structured data is the contracts created by a lawyer. It is common practice for lawyers to create what is called "boilerplate". This "boilerplate" is like a template that is utilized over and over. Only the client's name, date, and a few other details change from one contract to the next. As such, each contract is very similar to the next.

Textual structured data occurs fairly frequently. Textual structured data is found in medical records (especially laboratory results), real estate records, and elsewhere.

In case there is any confusion as to the differences between unstructured and structured textual data, consider this example:

Complaint 1:

My booking of Air Tkt (Through IRCTC web site) from Dharmshala to Delhi on 27th Dec got cancelled by AIR INDIA allowing full refund due to their operational difficulty, but IRCTC deducted an amount of 5220 considering airlines cancellation charge.

INDIAN RAILWAY CATERING & TOURISM CORPORATION LTD.

(A Government of India Enterprise)

Corporate Office: 9th Floor, Bank of Baroda Building, 16, Parliament Street, New Delhi-110001

Office Address: Internet Ticketing Centre, 1st Floor, State Entry Road, New Delhi-110055

PAN No: AAACI7074F, Service Tax Registration No. DL1/ST/RTA/15/2002

Txn Id: 5000941121 Kind Attn: KAMLENDU KUMAR Dated: 16-01-2015

Ref No: IRCTC Flight Booking No: FB1001041910

S. No. Pax. Name Can. Date. Sector / Flight Detail Ticket Amt.

Airline Can. Amt.

IRCTC Can. Amt.

Complaint 2:

I was denied a refund for baggage check charge of $25. I charged a companion ticket on my United Mileage Plus Explorer credit card for which I pay $95 a year. One of the benefits of having the card is to check your and your companion's bag free of charge. I submitted my refund request through

United's online 'baggage refund' site. I was credited the $25 for the outbound trip, however, they denied the inbound charge.

Complaint 3:

Was penalized $200.00 per ticket for emergency cancellation. Provided documentation regarding this to customer agent. He gave me an e-mail that was bogus to contact him.

Here there are three email complaints about airlines. These are examples of textual unstructured data.

Now consider the text from three contracts from the oil and gas industry:

Contract 1:

This Agreement is made and entered into this 21st day of May, 1994, by and between: Brewer Ranch, whose address is Hwy 7, Marathon, Texas hereinafter called Lessor (whether one or more), and Mobil, whose address is 54 Avenue Galleria, Houston, Texas, hereinafter called Lessee.

WITNESSETH, that the Lessor, for and in consideration of ONE THOUSAND ONE HUNDRED DOLLARS ($1100), cash in hand paid, the receipt and sufficiency of which are hereby acknowledged, and the covenants and agreements hereinafter contained, has...

Contract 2:

This Agreement is made and entered into this 10th day of October, 2004, by and between: Folmer Property, whose address is 12 First Street, Pampa, Texas, hereinafter called Lessor (whether one or more), and Vista Exploration Corporation, whose address is 1265 Tennis Club, Austin, Texas, hereinafter called Lessee.

WITNESSETH, that the Lessor, for and in consideration of ONE DOLLARS ($1),

cash in hand paid, the receipt and sufficiency of which are hereby acknowledged,...

Contract 3:

This Agreement is made and entered into this 15th day of January, 1998, by and between: Hardy Ranch, whose address is Hwy 10 Station B, Langtry,

Texas, hereinafter called Lessor (whether one or more), and Homer Exploration Corporation, whose address is 114 Irving Place, Dallas, Texas, hereinafter called Lessee.

WITNESSETH, that the Lessor, for and in consideration of TWO HUNDRED DOLLARS ($200), cash in hand paid, the receipt and sufficiency of which are hereby acknowledged, and the covenants and agreements hereinafter contained, has granted,...

Indeed there are differences between the contracts, but they are few and far between. This lawyer has created a contract where the business merely has to fill in the blanks. Much of the text is predictable. These contracts are examples of textual structured data. When considering structured textual data, it is often helpful to differentiate between repetitive "boilerplate" text and the text that is unique from one instance to the next.

This Agreement is made and entered into this 10th day of October, 2004, by and between: Folmer Property, whose address is 12 First Street, Pampa, Texas, hereinafter called Lessor (whether one or more), and Vista Exploration Corporation, whose address is 1265 Tennis Club, Austin, Texas, hereinafter called Lessee.

WITNESSETH, that the Lessor, for and in consideration of ONE DOLLARS ($1),

cash in hand paid, the receipt and sufficiency of which are hereby acknowledged,...

In this example, the plain text is consistent, while the text that is highlighted is the text that changes.

It's important to understand the difference between unstructured and structured textual data. Why? Because taxonomies are quite useful for unstructured textual data, but not as useful for structured data. The relevance of taxonomies to the different types of text becomes important when considering that in general, there is much more textual unstructured data than textual structured data in the world.

10: Textual Analytics

The conversion of text into actionable decisions can be achieved in many ways and in many contexts. One way text can be converted into a decision-making foundation is by creating a simple report or application:

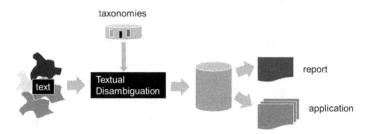

Here we see that raw text is fed through a textual disambiguation process. Taxonomies are used actively in the processing of the text. Output is created in a standard database format. Once the output is created, a report is created or an application is run. These reports and applications directly help organizations make important decisions based on their own data.

A report can be a one-time output, or it can be a regularly scheduled event. The distillation application can take the data distilled from the raw text and combine it with other data in order to create an analytical application. Both reports and applications are common products created from the conversion of raw text.

Another way to use the output derived from raw text is to put it into a data warehouse:

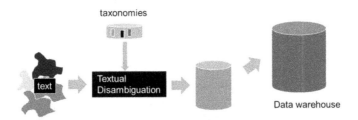

Storing data in a warehouse is convenient when the output of the textual disambiguation is highly compatible. There is no conversion or reformatting required. When the output is placed in a data warehouse, it can be combined and compared with previous outputs (as well as other types of data) to achieve broad perspectives and identify historical trends. On occasion there is a very large amount of data that is processed – too much to store in the data warehouse. In this case the output can be placed in a data lake. When data is placed into a data lake, it is contextualized, as follows:

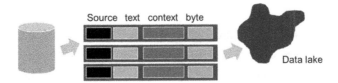

When contextualized, each piece of data has the following properties:

- **Source.** An identification of the source document. If there ever is a need to refer back to the originating source of the output, the connection can always be made.

- **Text.** The actual text from the document that has caught the attention of the textual analytics processor.

- **Context.** The context of the text as determined by the textual analytics processing.

- **Byte.** The actual byte address of the word in the originating source document. The byte address is useful if there ever is a need to return to the source document and find what the system was looking at in the textual analytics processing.

On occasion, it may be desirable to place BOTH the contextualized data and the raw text into the data lake. If there ever is a need to re-process the text, it is necessary to have the text stored in a contextualized format as well as stored in a raw text format.

The process of textual analysis is complex. When people use words, our brains automatically do a tremendous amount of complex background processing. When text is subjected to a computer, there's no brain sitting in the background waiting to process it. The computer must act as a brain to process and analyze text; to do this, it must be taught an incredible amount of complex logic.

The basic processing that occurs is textual disambiguation, which is the first step to accomplishing results with textual analytics. This is shown on the graphic on the facing page.

The starting point is raw text, and it can come from practically anywhere. It can come from newspapers, the internet, conversations, contracts, medical reports, speeches, customer feedback, and more. The text can be formal or informal. The text can be in any number of languages. As we've seen, taxonomies are derived from language itself. Taxonomies can be derived manually or can be acquired from a vendor.

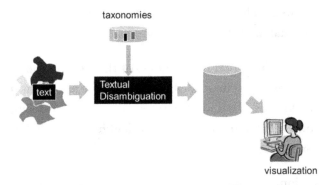

The technology of textual disambiguation is a mature technology that has hundreds of users and applications. The output of processing is a standard database that is compatible with all widely-used databases.

There are two basic paths through textual disambiguation: document fracturing and named value processing. Each of these paths employs very different methods.

DOCUMENT FRACTURING

When document fracturing is used to disambiguate text, the essential body of the document remains intact and is recognizable in the output:

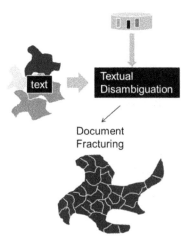

There are many components to document fracturing (which will be discussed at length in the next chapter).

NAMED VALUE PROCESSING

The other form of processing is termed "named value" processing:

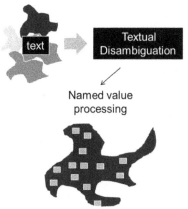

In named value processing, individual words and phrases are processed independently of the structure of the document. When examining the output of named value processing, you cannot easily discern what the original document looked like.

One way of thinking about document fracturing and named value processing is to imagine that in document fracturing you start at the first byte, process it, and move to the next byte. In named value processing, on the other hand, you search the entire document looking for strings of words and patterns.

SUPPORTING PROCESSES

Textual disambiguation doesn't stand on its own; there are many supporting processes that surround it.

MOVEREMOVE

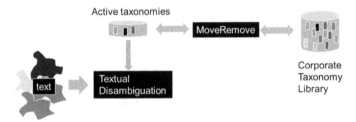

As a reminder, the MoveRemove module serves two essential purposes:

- To move taxonomies from the corporate taxonomy library to the active taxonomy area.
- To clean out the active taxonomy area after the execution of one type of document, in preparation for another type of document.

EMAIL FILTER MODULE

Another supporting process is the email filter module. When it comes time to process emails, you'll quickly realize that there is a lot of data to be processed, much of it unnecessary. Some emails are spam. Other emails are blather. And even for the relevant emails, there is a lot of system overhead data which is irrelevant to the message being conveyed. In order to keep the system from being overwhelmed, the email filter module filters emails before they ever get to textual disambiguation:

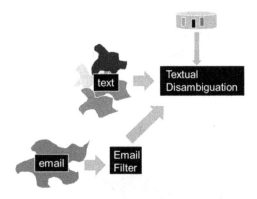

POSTPROCESS MERGE

Another really useful support module is the postprocess merge module. The outputs from named value processing and document fracturing are somewhat different. For many kinds of processes, this difference is not noticeable or really of interest. But some processes require that both named value processing and document fracturing run together. In this case, it is necessary to merge the outputs from the two types of processing. This merger of output occurs in the postprocess merge module:

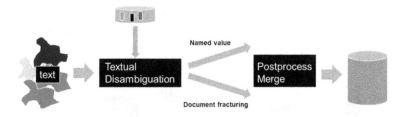

INDEPENDENT TAXONOMY CAPTURE MODULE

On occasion it is useful to work on more than one project at a time. In this case, the independent taxonomy capture program is helpful. The independent taxonomy capture program operates on the raw text, and interacts directly with the corporate taxonomy library. However, this module does *not* interact directly with the textual disambiguation program. This allows the taxonomy project to remain independent of the activities that occur within textual disambiguation:

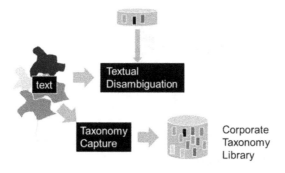

SECONDARY INFERENCE PROCESSING

A final and really important supporting module is the secondary inference processing module. In most cases, textual disambiguation systems can find and process whatever data they need simply by reading the raw text as presented. But because of inconsistent sentence structure and organization, it may be necessary to have a second pass at the data. This second pass is achieved by means of a secondary inference process:

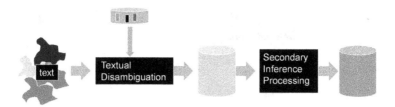

As an example of the need for secondary inference processing, consider the following sentence:

I like cake and ice cream.

This is a sentence about sentiment. It is easy enough to pick up the fact that the person likes cake, but ice cream is also in the scope of inference. In order to get the proper meaning out of this sentence, there need to be two inferences: that the person likes cake and that the person likes ice cream. In order to fully parse the meaning, a second inference pass of the data needs to be run.

There are many different kinds of inference that can be processed. Some of the other types of inference processing include negativity inference and note reconstruction.

11: Stage 1 Processing

At the heart of textual disambiguation lies the interpretation processing of raw text. Raw text is read into textual disambiguation and the interpreted text is written out to a database. This is what is referred to as "Stage 1" processing.

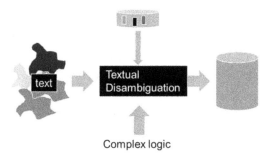

Complex logic

As we've previously discussed, textual disambiguation processes raw text against taxonomies using complex logic. This most basic step is known as "taxonomy processing," and is represented in the graphic on the next page.

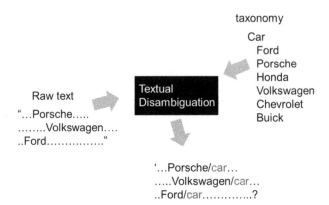

In basic taxonomy processing, raw text is read, and each word is compared to all of the specific words in the active taxonomy queue. When a specific word is encountered, a "hit" occurs. The hit causes the generic term to be applied to the specific term. In such a manner, taxonomies are applied to raw text.

Note that the taxonomy, at this point, is structured in the form of an ordered word pair.

The trickiest part of textual disambiguation is accounting for all the unpredictable variables that can be found in text. The logic that processes the text must account for all the unforeseen circumstances that may arise in the text. What follows are several examples of ways to make the most of taxonomy processing.

BASIC REFINEMENTS

In the previous example, it would be wise to include the specific word preceded by a blank space in the search logic. For example, " ford" instead of "ford". Including the blank space would avoid retrieving the word "afford".

Also note that the raw text is always searched as a lower case word. And any and all punctuations are removed. The raw text is searched as lower case in order to not misidentify a hit. For example, in the sentence "My Porsche runs fast." the word "Porsche" needs to be identified as "Porsche". Doing searches on a single case makes searching much more efficient. It has been observed that approximately 75% of raw text is served by these few basic refinements to taxonomy processing. The remaining 25% of text requires other techniques.

CUSTOM VARIABLES

Another very useful technique for interpreting text is the custom variable. Custom variables identify the context of a word by its actual structure. Most words have a mundane structure: several alphabetical characters combined. Other words, though, have more distinctive structures. When textual disambiguation encounters one of these words, it is easy to make the identification. This figure shows custom variable processing:

The term "JU9-8710" appears in the raw text. The system recognizes the word as a part number, because the custom variable has told it to look for the generic pattern "CC9-9999", where C indicates a capitalized letter, 9 represents any numeric digit, and "-" represents the symbol "-". Using this generic pattern, the system now knows the context of the word "JU9-8710".

INLINE CONTEXTUALIZATION

For structured, predictable text, it is possible to use inline contextualization to determine the meaning of a word or phrase. In inline contextualization, a beginning delimiter and an ending delimiter determine the context of a word or phrase. Here is an example of inline contextualization:

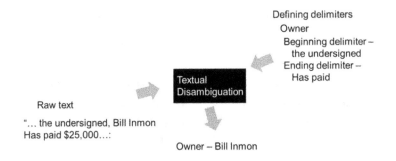

The example shows that the raw text identifies a gentleman known as Bill Inmon. The beginning delimiter is "the undersigned" and the ending delimiter is "has paid". Everything between the beginning delimiter and the ending delimiter is the "owner".

The applicability of inline contextualization is limited to structured textual information.

PROXIMITY ANALYSIS AND RESOLUTION

Sometimes when words are found in proximity to each other, they take on different meaning than if the words were separated. For this reason, there exist proximity variables. A proximity variable looks for words taken in proximity to each other and then makes a determination of their context. Here is an example of proximity analysis:

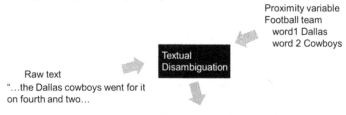

In this case the system looks for the words "Dallas" and "cowboys" in proximity to each other. When the system finds the words together, the system interprets the words to refer to a football team. If "Dallas" were in paragraph 1 and if "cowboys" were in paragraph 10, there would be a very different interpretation of the meaning of the text.

STOP WORD PROCESSING

Stop word processing removes all designated "stop" words. The English language is full of words that are extraneous. We need these words for proper communication, but they really don't have much (if any) bearing on what is being discussed. For that reason, these stop words are excised from the raw text. Here is an example of stop word processing:

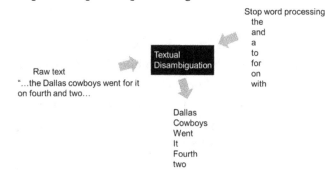

In the example, we see that the system has examined the text and has removed all the words that are on the stop word list. One reason to use stop word processing is to remove unnecessary words from the output database. This "paring down" of the text has many benefits. The largest benefit is to remove words that do not have any real value. By "paring down" the text, the remaining processing is streamlined.

ASSOCIATIVE WORD PROCESSING

On occasion, there arises a need to replace some word with another associated word. For example, in comparing contracts, one lawyer may use one set of terms while another lawyer uses another lexicon for the same subject. It is really beneficial to be able to understand that there indeed is a relationship between the two contracts, even though the precise words are different. This process is called associative word processing; it is illustrated in the following example:

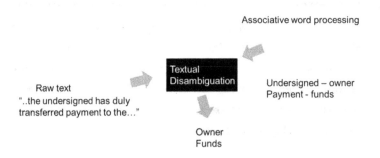

In the example, the system has been told that there is a relationship between the words "undersigned" and "owner", and between the words "payment" and "funds". The system reads the word "undersigned" and records a hit for "owner", and reads the word "payment" and interprets it as "funds".

HOMOGRAPHIC RESOLUTION

Another type of ambiguity that may arise in unstructured text is called homographic disambiguity. A homograph is similar to a homonym, with one key difference: homonyms are words that *sound* the same whereas homographs are words that are *spelled* the same.

A classical example of homographic disambiguity occurs in interpreting doctors' notes. Hypothetically, when the term "ha" is encountered in a doctor's text, it may refer to several things: heart attack, head ache, and hepatitis A, among others. The correct interpretation depends on who wrote the notes. If a cardiologist has written the notes, then ha refers to a heart attack. Here is an example of a homographic resolution:

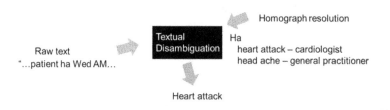

The system uses metadata to determine that this particular text has been written by a cardiologist. As such, the system determines ha to mean "heart attack".

ALTERNATE SPELLING

A common form of linguistic disambiguity is that of alternate spelling. The most common reason for differences in spelling is the difference in various English dialects (American, British, Australian, etc.). The next page contains an example of alternate spelling. In the example, the word "colour" is spelled in the British style. The system is instructed to change the spelling to the American style of spelling.

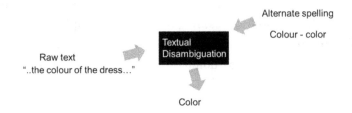

ACRONYM RESOLUTION

Another common source of ambiguity is acronyms. Acronyms are found everywhere; they are a common and normal form of communication. However, when it comes to textual disambiguation, it often makes sense to expand the acronym into its actual interpretation. Here is an example of acronym resolution:

In the example, the term "awol" is encountered in the raw text. The system knows to clarify the term "awol" as "away without official leave". Note that many different professions have their own set of acronyms and that there is considerable overlap between the different industries. This issue of which "awol" is the correct one is resolved by using the appropriate taxonomy with the correct data.

The analyst chooses the right set of terms to begin with. For example, consider the term "mvp". "Mvp" may refer to "most valuable player" or "Missouri Valley policeman". If the body of the data is about sports awards, the interpretation of "mvp" would probably be "most valuable player". But if the body of the text were about law enforcement, the interpretation of "mvp" probably would probably be "Missouri Valley policeman".

STEMMING

Another common form of linguistic disambiguity resolution is stemming. Stemming is the practice of reducing words to their Greek or Latin stems. For example, the words "moved", "moving", "mover", "moves" all have the common word stem "mov". Note that the "word stem" may or may not be an actual English word. Stemming is often useful in looking at text where the same word stem is found in many forms. Typically, conversations can best be analyzed by using stemming techniques.

Here is an example of stemming:

In the example, the raw text contains the words "leaving" and "blessed". The Latin word stems of these two words are "leav" and "bless".

DATE NORMALIZATION

Date can be written in many different formats. The method of choice may relate to geographical region, personal preference, or company protocol. In order to compare dates from different documents it is necessary to have a common and standard format for dates:

We see here that the date "July 13, 2016" is in the text. The date is read by textual disambiguation and is converted into the standard format as "20160713".

12: Stage 2 Processing

For many kinds of text, Stage 1 textual disambiguation is sufficient to create meaningful data and achieve sufficient results. In some cases, though, a complex sentence structure must be accommodated and data must be restructured so that it is in a more recognizable format. In these cases, a second stage called "secondary inference processing" can be helpful. Here we see that the output from textual disambiguation is passed through a secondary process, producing another, refined set of output:

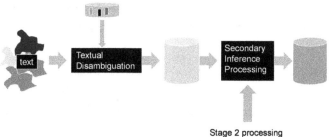

Stage 2 processing

There are three typical kinds of text that require secondary processing: sentiment analysis, negativity analysis, and medical records.

SENTIMENT ANALYSIS

The first kind of processing that can often be complicated enough to require Stage 2 processing is sentiment analysis. Sentiment analysis occurs when someone expresses an opinion about something. The opinion can be either positive or negative. In any case, the person making the expression wishes to make some kind of judgment about something.

Some simple examples of sentimental expressions are:

- I like you
- This ice cream is terrible
- The concert last night was terrible

In every case, there is a predicate that is being judged.

In order for sentiment analysis to be helpful, it must identify the predicate and then associate the sentiment with the predicate.

Normally making an association between a predicate and a judgment is a straightforward and easy thing to do. But things get to be more complicated when there are two or more predicates. Consider the following simple expression:

I like cake and ice cream.

```
Like cake
Like ice cream
```

While the sentence is simple, there are actually two predicates in this sentence: cake and ice cream. Making the association between "like" and "cake" is easy to do. Where things become a little more complex is in terms of "like" and "ice cream". The reason why the association between "like" and "ice cream" is more challenging is because words have to be processed in an order that is not sequential – something that's not logical for a computer. This is why secondary processing of text is required.

The sentence in the example is a very simple sentence. It needs to be recognized that here are many sentences that are a lot more complex than the one seen in the example, such as "I love this restaurant but I hate this dish."

NEGATIVITY ANALYSIS

In the same vein as sentiment analysis is negativity analysis. This type of Stage 2 processing requires the system to recognize that something is not being expressed. Consider the following negative expressions:

- You cannot go out
- The tumor was not malignant
- The cat does not have claws

In each of these sentences there is an expression of something that is not occurring or is not going to happen. But sentences can be much more complex than those found in the three examples. Consider this sentence:

She doesn't have any money or talent.

```
Doesn't have any money
Doesn't have any talent
```

Here we have two negative expressions:

- She doesn't have any money
- She doesn't have any talent

Making the first association is easy to do. Making the second association is more difficult, again, because the words have to be processed out of order. That is why a secondary level of processing is needed.

In both sentiment analysis and in negativity analysis, there is a logical construct that needs to be created for the sentences in question. These logical constructs are the scope of sentiment and the scope of negation. There needs to be an understanding that when people make sentences, their sentiment extends to the entire scope of sentiment or the entire scope of negativity. Scope refers to the linguistic practice of inference until end of sentence. For example, take this sentence: "I do not like ice cream, cake, or cookies." The sentiment "do not like" refers to everything mentioned until the period is encountered.

Both the scope of sentiment and the scope of negativity can be called scopes of inference. It is in the secondary inference processing step that the scopes of inference are applied.

MEDICAL RECORDS

Another place where secondary processing is required is when considering medical records. Whenever a patient seeks treatment, an assessment is made. In every scenario, from a simple sports physical to an emergency surgery, records are required for legal, ethical, and practical reasons.

The facing page contains an example of a typical medical record. The record is a statement of the events that occurred during the medical encounter. Note that the format of the record is narrative. Narrative is good for humans reading the record, but is almost worthless when it comes to the recording of the record for computer analytical purposes.

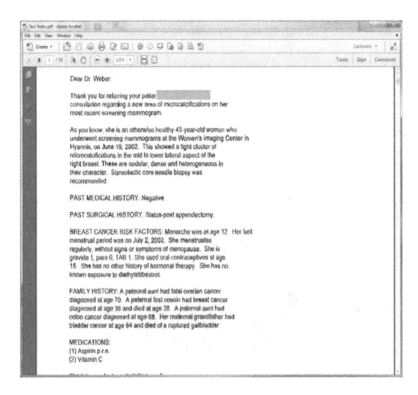

It is easy enough to process the narrative using textual disambiguation:

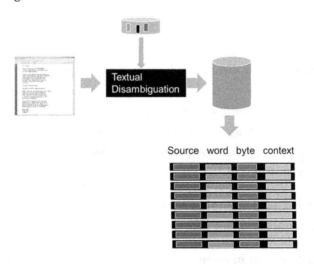

The output textual disambiguation is a simple relational file of data. This output file is useful for many kinds of processing, but most medical professionals would be stymied by the output. It just would not look like anything they would use.

SECONDARY INFERENCE PROCESSING OF THE MEDICAL RECORD

In order to make the output more useful and more palatable to the medical analyst, secondary inference processing is needed. This figure shows how the output from Stage 1 processing is passed to secondary inference processing:

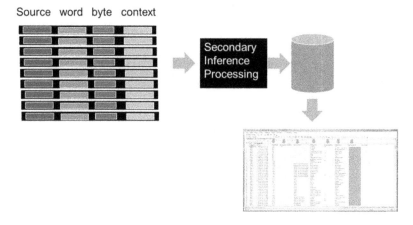

The output from secondary inference processing is a relational database. However, it's no ordinary relational database. This relational database has been tailored to meet the needs of the data analyst doing particular analytical work on medical records. This is how powerful text processing can be when properly customized to fit user needs!

The facing page contains a closer look at the output that has been generated by this particular secondary inference program.

The first column in essentially every medical database identifies the source of the medical record. If there ever is any question

about the accuracy or content of the relational database, each
entry can be tied directly back to its origin.

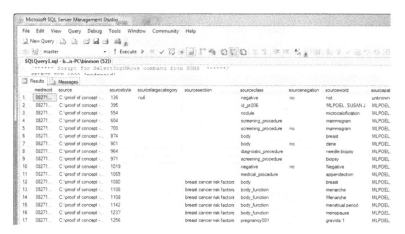

The second column in the database is the byte address where
the word can be found in the source document. The byte
address is useful for at least two purposes: to allow reference to
precisely where in the source document the word originated
from, and to be able to restructure the relational database in the
order in which the doctor actually wrote the document.

The third column in the report is the "super classification"
column. A super classification indicates that the doctor has
organized comments according to a broad category. For
example, the doctor might sort comments into "plan of
treatment" or "surgical history" or "general observations".
These would all be super classifications of data. In this example,
there are no super classifications.

The fourth column contains sub-classifications of text. In the
sub-classifications, the doctor might organize text according to
specific areas of interest: nose, skin, neck, stomach, etc. In the
previous example, the first few items do not have a sub-
classification, but the next set of items do have a sub-
classification.

The next column shows the classification of the word in question. There are many ways to classify words found in a medical report. The analyst may choose to use a taxonomy. Or the analyst may choose to use a classification from an industry publication like ICD 10 or Snomed. The analyst will choose the best option based on the medical report and how it will be analyzed.

The next column is the negation column. If the doctor has said that something doesn't exist, then the word "no" is found in this column. For example, if the doctor said "There was no malignant tumor." Then the word "no" would be attached to "tumor".

The next column indicates the word itself that has been lifted from the medical report.

The final column is the name or identification of the patient. For the purposes of this book, the full name of the patient has been cropped out of this screenshot. The result of organizing the data this way is that the relational database, when sorted by source and byte, closely resembles the actual report as written by the doctor. A doctor can read the relational database and recognize that it has come from the medical report issued by the doctor. The facing page contains the same report in two formats.

Every element found in the medical report is recognizable within the relational database. The close resemblance of the relational database to the narrative medical record makes the relational database easy and intuitive to analyze.

Although it isn't obvious to the casual observer, the medical record as arranged in the relational database is very easy for the analyst to use. Here is the string of information contained in each row of the relational database:

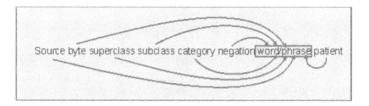

Each row is a composite of relevant data. The analyst needs to see each of the elements of data that exist in the row.

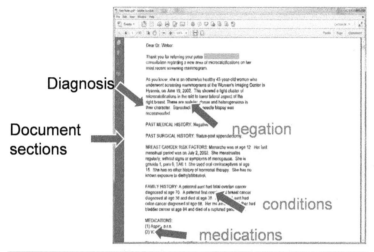

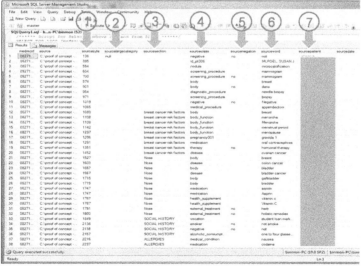

13: Banking Analytics

The world of text analytics is full of opportunity in every industry. Wherever there is a competitive marketplace and wherever there are customers with opinions, there is opportunity to use textual analytics. The value of text analytics in many cases is to allow an organization to hear the voices of their customers. Hearing what a customer has to say is invaluable. Once the organization knows what is on the mind of the customer, the organization can then tailor their products or services to better accommodate the customer. This improved service creates loyal customers. One industry where this is readily apparent is the banking industry.

PUBLICLY AVAILABLE BANKING DATA

One good place to hear what customers are saying is the internet. On the internet there are a lot of places where customers can voice their feelings, as complaints or compliments. Over time, a whole host of banking customer feedback records in a narrative format have been accumulated.

COMMENTS COLLECTED

In this case study, the records that were accumulated expressed everything from the simplest sentiments to the most virulent of emotions. It was common for a complaint to mention more than one topic, although some did not. Some of the complaints were short and succinct, and other complains were lengthy and verbose.

In every case, the feedback from the banking customers mentioned which aspect(s) of banking the customer was opinionated about.

Here is an example of one of the complaints found on the Internet:

I banked with Susquehanna for over ten years with no issue. From takeover forward... I am dealing with issues still not resolved. They are unable to find a deposit made to my account. I have spoken with many reps and my account was to be noted it was being researched. They charged off my account to check systems due to their mistake and still it is unresolved and I am weekly speaking with them! I face having a new account with another bank closed in the meantime and as a single mom of two this is creating a serious hardship.

In all, over 2,000 complaints were gathered for four banks: BB&T, Bank of America, Chase Bank, and US Bank. These banks were chosen because they were representative of the banking industry as a whole.

Once this large body of publicly available text was gathered from the internet, the next step was to choose a taxonomy that reflected banking customer sentiment. Here is a sample of the taxonomy that was chosen:

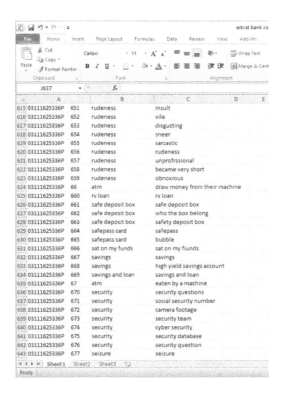

Note that the taxonomy was in the form of ordered word pairs, stored in a simple relational database. Once the taxonomy had been selected and stored in a simple database, the processing of the text was ready to commence.

TEXTUAL DISAMBIGUATION

The next step was to run the text through textual disambiguation using the taxonomy as input:

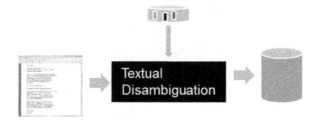

The result of this processing was a simple relational table:

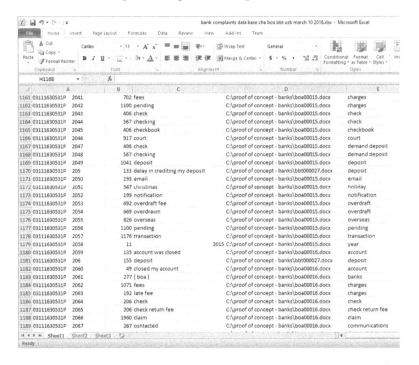

The table was a big step toward producing a useful analytical result – but only the first step. In a way, the table that has been produced reduces the text to a database. But there is still other processing needed in order to make meaningful analytical insights.

SECONDARY INFERENCE ANALYSIS

The normalized text is useful, but it still does not serve the purposes of sentiment analysis. In order to be useful for analytical processing, a second processing step is needed. The normalized data must be run through inference processing as follows:

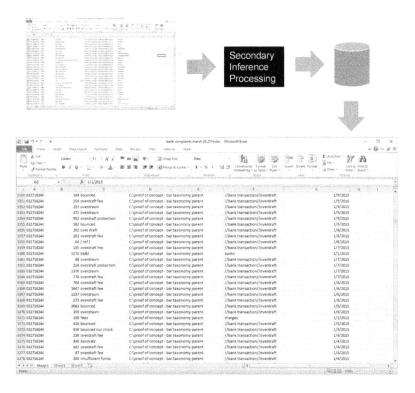

The output of this secondary inference processing is another relational table.

VISUALIZATION

The stage is now set to turn the processed text into an analytical visualization – the third major step of textual analysis. The following figure shows how the inference-processed text is entered into a visualization/dashboard software package. (Note: This visualization was produced by Boulder Insight Group.)

The output is a dashboard that shows many important aspects of the publicly available data that was analyzed.

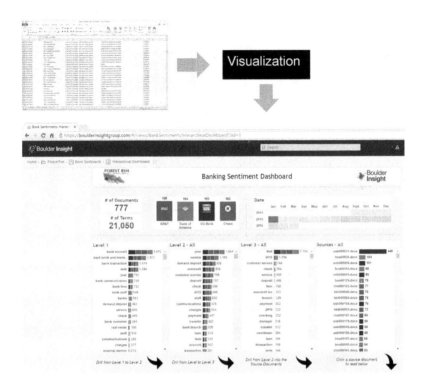

INTERPRETING THE DASHBOARD

Now, let's take a look at our final, visualized results. The first thing of interest is which banks specifically have participated in the study. The figure on the facing page shows the symbols for the banks. The banks that were chosen for representation in the study were BB&T, Bank of America, US Bank, and Chase Bank. Each of the banks is represented by its own unique color and symbol in the report.

The next item of interest is the list of subjects that were on the mind of the customers. The first column to the left shows the topics mentioned by the banks' customers. The topics are ranked according to the frequency of mention. In addition, the mentions are color-coded so that the analyst can see which bank generated which mention.

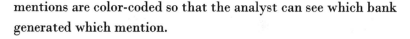
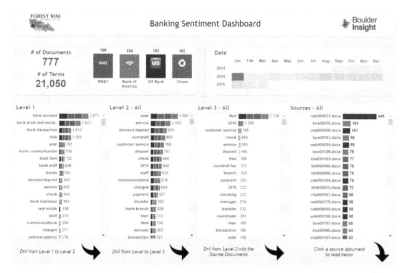

It is worth noting that this graphic depiction only shows the top subjects. In the actual dashboard, it is possible to review each and every topic mentioned in the bank customer feedback.

The next column to the right is the "drill down" column. In this column, you can see all the drill down information that was captured by the taxonomy.

As a simple example of the drill down capability, the column on the left may have had the term "bank employee" and the column next to it may have "teller". In such a fashion, the analyst can drill down on all of the topics mentioned in the banks' customer feedback.

Finally, we reach the ultimate in drill down capability. In the rightmost column you can see the actual comment that caused the mention to register in the dashboard.

Here we see what one of the actual comments looks like:

Oct. 16, 2015
Satisfaction Rating

On Wednesday, September 30th an investigator from Adult Protection Services came to my home unannounced. My caregiver let him in and he asked to talk to me. The investigator told me that someone from Chase reported that my caregiver cashed checks from me that over the last 4 months that had "Landscaping" in the comment line. He said in that 4 month period those checks totaled $20,000. I explained that before I

Drilling down is accomplished by right clicking on the phrase. Drill down is a feature of the software tool used to build the visualization.

CONSIDERING A SINGLE BANK

A final useful feature of the dashboard is the capability to hone in on one bank in particular. As previously mentioned, the default view includes data from all banks in the study. But if you want to look at comments from just one bank, you can do so by selecting the icon for the bank of interest, as in this figure:

14: Call Center Analytics

How many organizations have a customer service phone number that you can call? Nearly all of them. And what kinds of conversations take place on these "800" numbers? There are many topics:

- Complaints
- Questions about installing equipment
- Questions about other products
- Requests to buy more products
- Clarification of instructions
- Questions about deliveries and locations

In many ways, the customer service line reflects the voice of the consumer in a direct and unedited manner. This "unfiltered" information provided by the consumer is nothing short of invaluable. Yet what do organizations do with the conversations that come in on their 800 number? In most cases, the conversations are simply thrown away. Occasionally, the conversations are recorded then put in an archive which almost never is accessed.

The voice of the customer is alive and well...and being ignored by the organization.

But ask a manager if they know what is going on in a call center, and the manager will say, "yes, we know what is going on in our call center". Then the manager will then tell you: "We have 5,000 calls a day and the calls last an average of 6 ½ minutes."

The manager that claims that they know what is going on in the call center has missed the whole point of the call center. Certainly the number of the calls and the length of the calls are interesting measurements, but they do not say anything about what is on the minds of the customers.

In today's world, you *can* know what is on the mind of your customers. You *can* hear what the customer is saying. You just need to listen.

WHAT THE CALL CENTER HEARS

Consider the record of information received by one call center, shown on the facing page. On the right side of this report is a column called "narrative". In the narrative column is found a brief summary of the conversation that has occurred between a representative of the organization and a customer. In this example, there were approximately 75,000 phone conversations a day. That is a far greater number than could ever be processed manually.

Instead, the textual interchanges were put into a file and used as input for textual disambiguation/textual ETL.

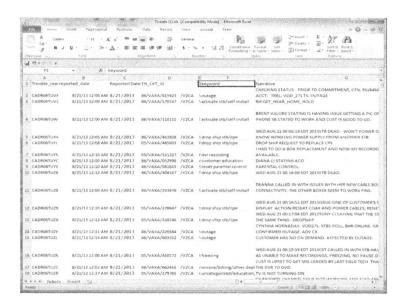

PROCESSING THE NARRATIVE

The text is then processed as follows:

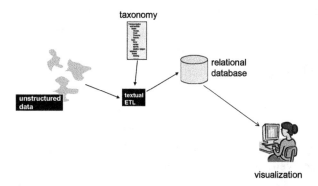

The text is first fed into textual ETL. A taxonomy that is suited for analyzing call center information is applied, and a relational database is created. Then the relational database is fed into visualization/analytical software. Here are the results of the visualization (dashboard created by Boulder Insight Group):

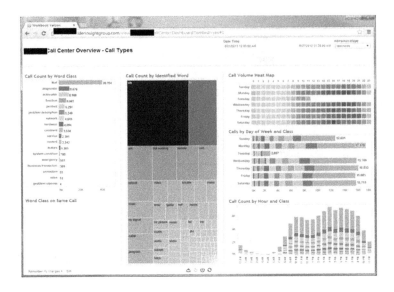

EXAMINING THE DASHBOARD

In the dashboard, in the top-left portion, there is a general characterization of the conversations that have occurred. The conversations are ranked by the number of occurrences of conversations there have been. At a glance, management can see the most common types of conversations that have been received by their call center.

To the bottom-right of the dashboard is a demograph of the conversations versus the time of day when the conversations transpired. Not surprisingly, at 2:00 am there are not many calls received. But by 10:00 am, there is a lot more call volume. Furthermore, the conversations are color-coded. This allows the analyst to "drill down" on the conversations that have occurred at any one moment in time. Above the hourly analysis are daily and monthly analyses. Here the analyst can see the relative amount of calls on different days of the week and days throughout the month. The different colors refer to the type of comment being made. Complaints are one color. Questions are another color. Installation requests are another color, and so forth. Finally, the centerpiece of the dashboard is a map of the subjects that were discussed in the conversations. In the largest black box is the subject that was discussed the most – in this case "stb", which is an acronym for "set up box". The next biggest square represents the next most common topic, and so on. This dashboard clearly helps management to really know what is being discussed in the call center. Textual disambiguation (with the help of taxonomies) coupled with visualization has created a powerful analytic tool upon which to base important decisions.

GETTING TO VISUALIZATION

Although the visualized dashboard is the most useful product, it is more interesting to examine the processing that was required to get there. The original raw input to the computer was a single, flat string of characters:

Through the algorithms found in textual ETL and the appropriate taxonomies, this raw and unintelligible text was transformed into a database. We discussed several algorithms earlier in this book, and you can see where quite a few of them were used in this instance of textual analytical processing:

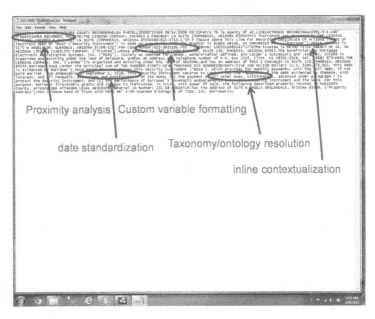

With the help of these algorithms, the raw string of text was converted into a standard database, as shown on the facing page.

As usual, the essential elements of the database include:

- The document source
- The byte the word being analyzed is found at
- The word itself
- The context of the word

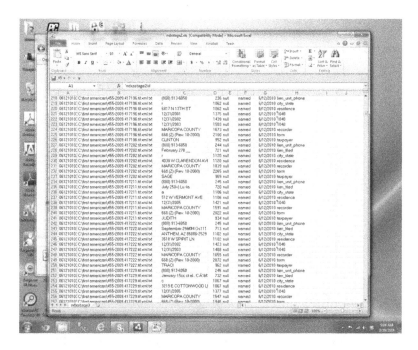

The most interesting of this data that has been derived from the document is the context of the word itself:

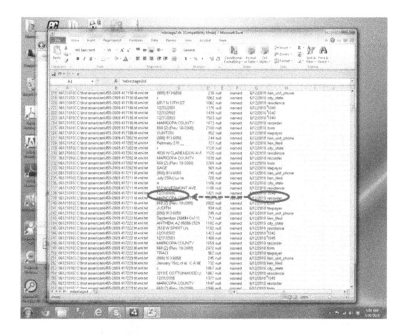

For every word identified from the raw text, there has been context identified.

15: Hospitality Analytics

The restaurant business is as competitive as any other. Restaurants are always competing for new customers as well as fighting to hold on to their existing "regulars". In order to achieve these goals, restaurants must strive for excellence, which can be measured by any number of parameters:

- Menu
- Ambience
- Service
- Pricing

While there are other aspects to managing a restaurant, these factors are typically the most important to customers. Therefore, these are some of the key measurements needed to analyze sentiment in the restaurant business and other parts of the hospitality industry.

VOICE OF THE CUSTOMER

Success in managing a restaurant always boils down to one thing: the opinion of the customer. The restaurant can rate itself all it wants, but the only opinion that really counts is that of the customer.

For long-term success and growth, the restaurant needs to listen continuously to the feedback of its customers. It is not enough for the restaurant to hear the voice of the customer today. The restaurant must hear the voice of the customer tomorrow, next week, and next month. There are many ways the restaurant can gather feedback. Until recently, one of the most common methods was to collect paper comment cards placed at every table. But in today's world, feedback is most commonly shared online. Whether on the restaurant's specific webpage, or on a generic ratings website like Yelp, customers often don't hesitate to voice their compliments and complaints.

It's no wonder why the internet has become a popular medium to share feedback. From behind a computer or mobile screen, customers can choose to remain anonymous. Similarly, anonymity may prompt customers to be more honest or even explicit. Customers can write as long or short a message as they want.

As a simple example of feedback given to a restaurant, consider the following contrived comment:

Product(s): Caesar Salad Parmesan Chicken Breast I have ordered a Caesar Salad with a Parmesan Chicken Breast twice now. Both times, the restaurant neglected to include the chicken in my to go order. Also, today I was given dressing that had separated. I called and was told that that's just how it was going to be. I love your restaurant and was very disappointed. Not a good experience at all.

Over time, a restaurant will receive many messages similar to this one. There are many lessons to be learned from this customer feedback, but only if the restaurant knows how to navigate some technical hurdles first.

The first problem is that there is an overwhelming quantity of comments. In a month's time there may 50,000 to 100,000 messages for a good sized restaurant chain. Trying to manually read and digest 50,000 messages manually is an impossible task.

The second issue is that the messages are in raw text format. As we've seen, computers generally do not handle text well. Thankfully, though, we now know how to turn this wall of text into useful information.

ANALYZING RESTAURANT FEEDBACK

Once again, textual disambiguation is the first step toward making sense of all of this customer feedback:

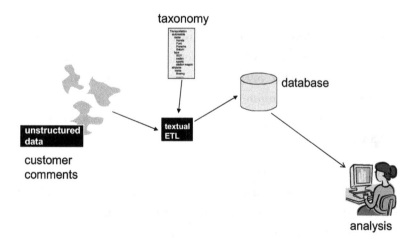

Textual data (customer comments) are fed into textual disambiguation. You can feed as many as you like into textual disambiguation, and the comments are in text narrative format. Textual disambiguation then reads, analyzes, and converts the comments into a database. Once the comments have been converted into a database, they can then be analyzed by a standard analytical program. Then management can see what the customer is saying.

Here is an example of what a visualization product created by analyzing restaurant feedback text might look like:

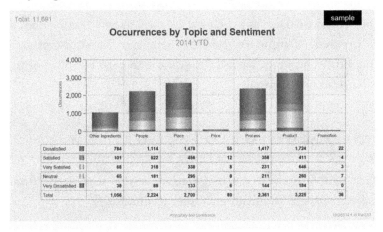

The graph shows evaluation of seven categories: other ingredients, people, place, price, process, product and promotions. On this particular visualization, red and purple indicate negative comments while blue and green indicate positive experiences. At first glance, it appears that this restaurant is not doing so well.

But industry experience has shown that under normal circumstances, people are much more likely to give feedback when they are dissatisfied. Some industry experts anticipate that the ratio of bad to good experiences reported is 85% to 15%. For this reason, the alarming quantity of red is not necessarily unexpected.

There is one really remarkable fact that sticks out from this chart: hardly anyone has commented on price. This is an indication that the restaurant chain is "leaving money on the table". The restaurant chain may need to consider marginally raising prices.

Another interesting fact that comes from this graph is that hardly anyone has anything to say about promotions. You might assume that this means the restaurant chain isn't running any promotions, but in this case, they actually were. This indicates that the promotions are having little or no impact; the restaurant ought to reconsider them.

Here's another visualization that was gleaned from this data:

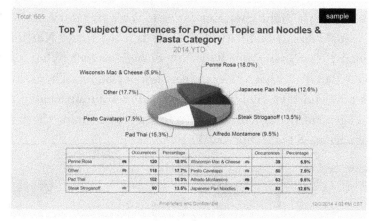

This graph shows different dishes in the pasta category. The most frequently mentioned dish was penne rosa and the least commonly mentioned dish was Wisconsin macaroni and cheese.

But the information goes deeper than that. If the manager wants to, they can "drill down" on any given dish. For example, take a closer look at the customers' thoughts on Pad Thai:

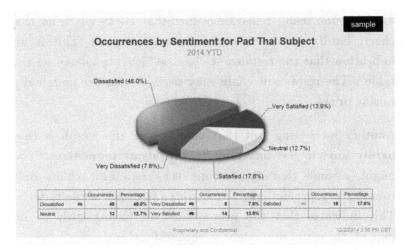

When you drill down on this particular dish, you see that most of the comments were expressing dissatisfaction. This empowers you to ask the right questions to try to solve this problem: why are people dissatisfied with Pad Thai? Is it too spicy? Not spicy enough? Too many noodles? Not enough sauce? What is it about Pad Thai that the customers are not liking? Thankfully, the powerful text analytics used by this restaurant enable the management to "drill down" even further, to examine the exact language used regarding Pad Thai:

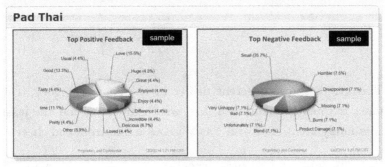

It is now very evident exactly how the customers feel about the Pad Thai. On the negative side, it seems that portion size is the main criticism. The restaurant needs to increase the portion size of Pad Thai in order to please their customers. This very specific and direct feedback is invaluable to the management. There are

still more powerful pieces of information that can be gathered
from the customers' feedback, such as the graph below. This
visualization shows feedback over time. If the restaurant was
testing a new recipe over a period of a couple months, or if there
was a string of particularly rainy days, the restaurant could
compare sentiments from a specific period to the general
average.

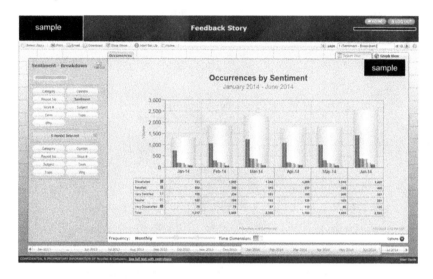

Another possibility is looking at customer feedback by store
locations – particularly useful for restaurant chains:

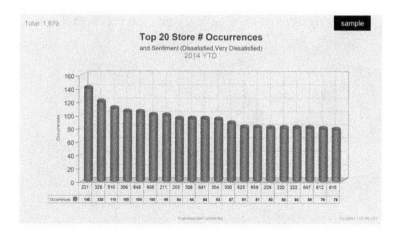

In this case, it is clear that store 221 has had more feedback than any other store. This may or may not be an indicator of a problem at store 221. It could be that store 221 is in mid-town Manhattan and does more business than any other store. Or it could be a sign that store 221 is the source of a lot of complaints. If this information were married with other corporate information, you could determine which scenario is more likely, and take appropriate action. In fact, by "drilling down," the management can find out what exactly is going on in location 221:

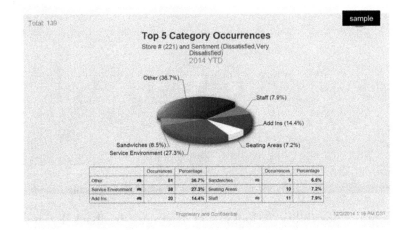

If management is looking for problems to solve, these visualizations have given them very powerful tools to do so.

16: Airline Analytics

As our final case study, we'll examine the extremely competitive world of airlines. There are fare wars. There are frequent flyer clubs. There are airline lounges at major airports. There are new routes being opened up. There are special seat pricing algorithms.

At the end of the day, all that matters to an airline is the customer and which company the customer chooses for his or her journey. And through the power of making choices, customers ultimately determine the economic success of airlines.

Therefore, in order to become successful, an airline must listen to its customers. Listening to customers is simple in concept, but as we've seen throughout this book, complex in execution. Once again, there are several factors that make this a difficult task:

- Large volume of customers
- Many outlets for the customers to express themselves

- Computers are designed for handling transactions, not language

It is simply not possible for any airline's customer service representatives to listen, one at a time, to what each and every passenger has to say about their flight.

Thankfully, as we've seen, collecting feedback online is an extremely practical alternative. And airline passengers have made great use of it – there exist plenty of websites solely dedicated to airline complaints:

In the spring of 2016, Forest Rim Technology gathered up a large collection of passenger feedback forms from a wide variety of websites. The information that was gathered was open to the public. Forest Rim assembled the comments into a textual data set.

The dataset comprised passenger feedback for the entirety of the year for 2015 and the spring of 2016. All airlines were included, and the comments included both domestic (U.S.) and worldwide flights. There was no effort to either include or exclude the complaints for any airline.

Here's just one example of a typical comment:

On 31.01.2016 I landed at Delhi airport on flight number AI 116 at 2:50am. Unfortunately my baggage did not arrive.

I inquired at the airport and was told that my baggage will arrive at my hotel at 3pm the same day as my luggage was on another flight.

I waited at my hotel until 3pm and my luggage had not arrived. I contacted Air India at Delhi airport and I was told it would arrive at my hotel at 6pm. At 6pm the luggage had still not arrived at my hotel so I contacted Air India at Delhi airport and I was told that it would arrive at my hotel at 9pm. At 9pm the luggage had still not arrived at my hotel so I contacted Air India at Delhi airport and I was told it would arrive at my hotel 9am the next morning. At 9am the next morning my luggage had still not arrived at my hotel.

The raw text of all of this feedback was processed in the same manner we've seen several times now:

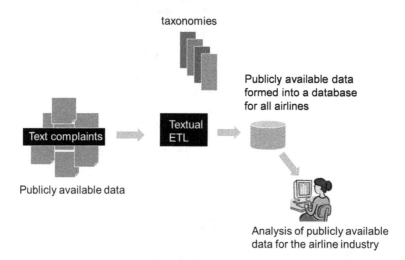

Yet again, textual disambiguation coupled with taxonomies appropriate to airlines passengers did the heavy lifting, creating a database. A visualization was then created for analysis.

Here's a snapshot of the resulting visualization by Boulder Insight:

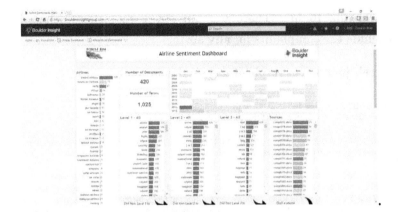

The first column shows the airlines that were mentioned and the order of frequency in which they were mentioned:

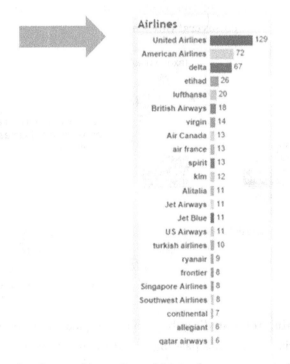

The second column shows the subjects that were mentioned by the passengers, ranked once again by the number of times they were mentioned:

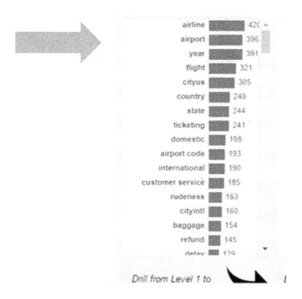

Drill from Level 1 to

The third column shows the sub-rankings for any given column.

As with all visualization dashboards, there are many ways to examine the data. One method is to focus on one airline in particular, then to focus on one aspect of that airline:

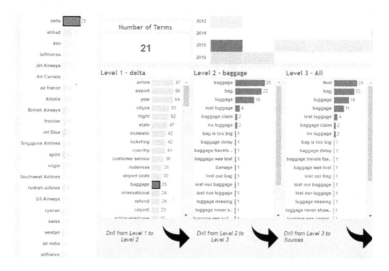

In this case, the airline chosen was Delta Airlines and the subject of interest was luggage. The second column shows the comments made about luggage handling at Delta Airlines.

Once again, analysts can "drill down" through many levels or layers of data, all the way to the actual comment that was used to create the analysis in the first place:

Product: flight cancellation

Company: Delta Airlines

Category: Airlines

Hello,

I'm writing to find out the most effective way of filing a complaint about Delta Airlines.

My name is Basak O, and I am a business traveler who uses Delta's services frequently. However, my latest experience with Delta has been exhausting, disappointing, and painful. I was supposed to be on Delta Flight Number 148 on December 19, 2009, however, due to weather conditions, my flight was canceled. My Delta number was DYOK36. I had to miss a very important meeting; I suffered financial loses; and I was very upset at the rudeness of the Delta personnel at JFK. Then they put me on a direct flight to Istanbul on December 20, 2009, *which was canceled not because of the weather but because the flight attendants could not make it to the airport. Upon hearing this disappointing news, I went to collect my baggage from Delta, but they were unable to find it, although they did make me wait for five hours at JFK. They finally told me that my luggage would be waiting for me in Istanbul. I wanted to speak with a Delta representative to cancel my flight and collect my money back, but there was absolutely no one available. Furthermore, no one picked the telephone for 72 hours at Delta!*

Since the beginning of the computer industry, textual data has been largely ignored. This is an incredible shame, because there is clearly so much business value to be found in textual data. This book has explored the subject of textual ETL and taxonomies in great depth. It is hoped that this book will be your guide to opening up whole new worlds of opportunity to turn textual data in to real business value – almost like alchemy.

Glossary

Acronym resolution – the process of expanding acronyms into their literal meanings

Accuracy – a qualitative assessment of freedom from error or a quantitative measurement of the magnitude of error

Active taxonomy – the taxonomy or taxonomies used in active execution of textual disambiguation

Algorithm – the instructions that govern the flow of activity in a procedure

Alternate spelling – a different way of forming a word pattern

Alternate storage – storage other than disk-based storage used to hold bulk amounts of data

Associative word processing – processing of words with the understanding that some words have alternates

Attribute – a value of data that is distinguishable from other values

Blather – email message that has no business relevance

Contextualization – the process of identifying the context of a word

Corporate taxonomy library – a collection of all the taxonomies relevant to and useful to the organization

Curated taxonomy – a prefabricated taxonomy; a generic taxonomy

Custom variable – a string of data whose type is recognizable merely from the structure of the string

Dashboard – data visualization tools that display the numbers, metrics and scorecards on a single screen, making it easy for a business person to get information from difference sources and customize the appearance

Database – a structured collection of units of data organized around some topic or theme

Database key – a data used for identification of a record

Database server – a computer dedicated to the execution of database commands

Data definition – the process of defining the semantics of data

Data dictionary – a repository of the metadata useful to the organization

Data lake – a byproduct of "Big Data"; the place where large quantities of data are stored

Data mining – analysis of large quantities of data to find patterns such as groups of records, unusual records and dependencies

Data model – an abstraction of data

Data warehouse – a subject oriented, integrated, non-volatile, time variant collection of data in support of management's decisions

Deadly embrace – the locking of a system in which one process wants to access data held by another process at the same time that the other process is trying to access data protected by the first process

DIS (data item set) – the middle level of a data model

Discriminating criteria – the criteria that determines whether text either belongs in a taxonomy or does not belong in a taxonomy

Document fracturing – in textual disambiguation, the process of sequentially processing text looking for text that satisfies such criteria as stop word processing, stemming, homographic resolution, and more

Domain – set or range of valid values for a variable

Generic element – a taxonomic classification of a broad class of elements

Metadata – self-referential information; commonly known as "data about the data"

MoveRemove process – a program that manages the movement of taxonomies back and forth from the active taxonomy to the corporate taxonomy library

Negative taxonomy – a taxonomy containing terms of negation: no, not, never, none, hardly, etc.

Negativity analysis – the analysis of a sentence where a term of negation has been used

Ontology – a logical relationship of elements participating in a taxonomy

Preferred taxonomy – the taxonomy that is first in line in the process of taxonomy resolution

Proximity analysis – an analysis based on the closeness of words or taxonomies to each other in a textual document

Sentiment processing – the analysis of the feelings expressed in a sentence

Stemming – the reduction of words to their root. For example, the stem of moving, moved, mover, and move is the stem "mov".

Stop word – a word in a language that is needed for communication but not needed to convey information. For example, "a", "and", "the", "to", and "from".

Tableau – a popular visualization tool

Tagging – the process of searching text for predetermined words

Taxonomy – a classification of text

Taxonomy resolution – the process of matching raw text to a taxonomy by examining the specific elements of the taxonomy

Text analytics – the process of reducing text into a form where management decisions can be made from the contents of the text

Textual disambiguation – the process of reading text and formatting text into a standard database format

Textual ETL – see textual disambiguation

Unstructured data – data whose logical organization is not apparent to the computer

References

Inmon, W.H. *Data Architecture – A Primer for the Data Scientist*. Elsevier Kauffman, 2013.

Inmon, W.H. *DW 2.0 – Architecture for the Next Generation of Data Warehousing*. June 2008.

Inmon, W.H. *Building the Data Warehouse*. QED, 1990.

Inmon, W.H. *Building the Unstructured Data Warehouse*. Technics Publications, 2011.

Inmon, W.H. *Data Lake Architecture*. Technics Publications, 2016.

Kaufmann, M. and Krishnan, K. *Data Warehouse in the Age of Big Data*. 2005.

Kaufmann, M. and Krishnan, K. *Social Data Analytics*. 2009.

Inmon, W.H. and Wiley, John. *Exploration Warehousing: Turning Information into Business Opportunity*. 2000.

Inmon, W.H. with Nesavich, Tony. *Tapping Into Unstructured Data*. Prentice Hall, 2007.

Multiple whitepapers by Forest Rim Technology Inc. were consulted. These can be retrieved from www.forestrimtech.com.

Index

www.ingramcontent.com/pod-product-compliance
Lightning Source LLC
Chambersburg PA
CBHW071252050326
40690CB00011B/2368